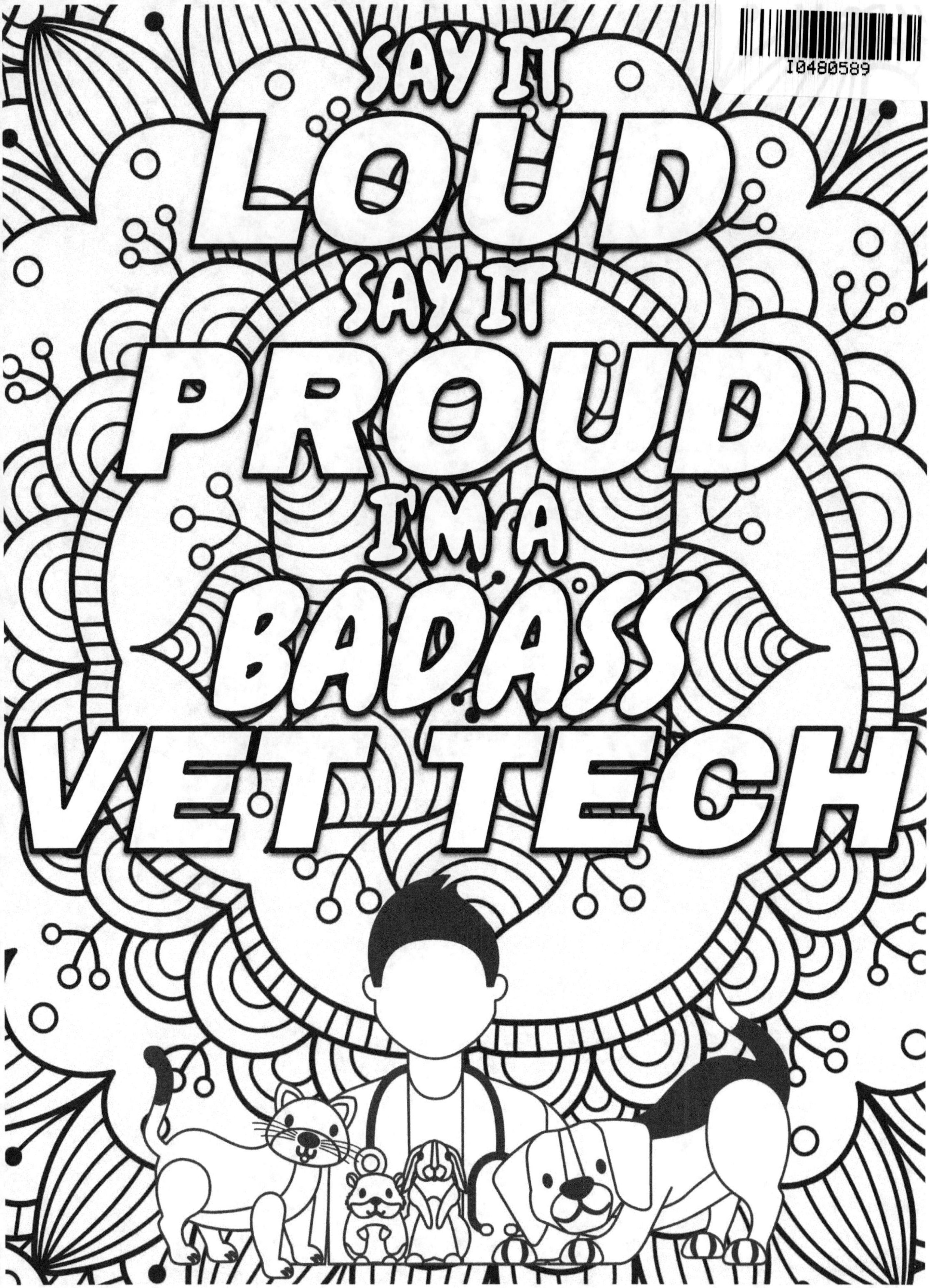
SAY IT
LOUD
SAY IT
PROUD
I'M A
BADASS
VET TECH

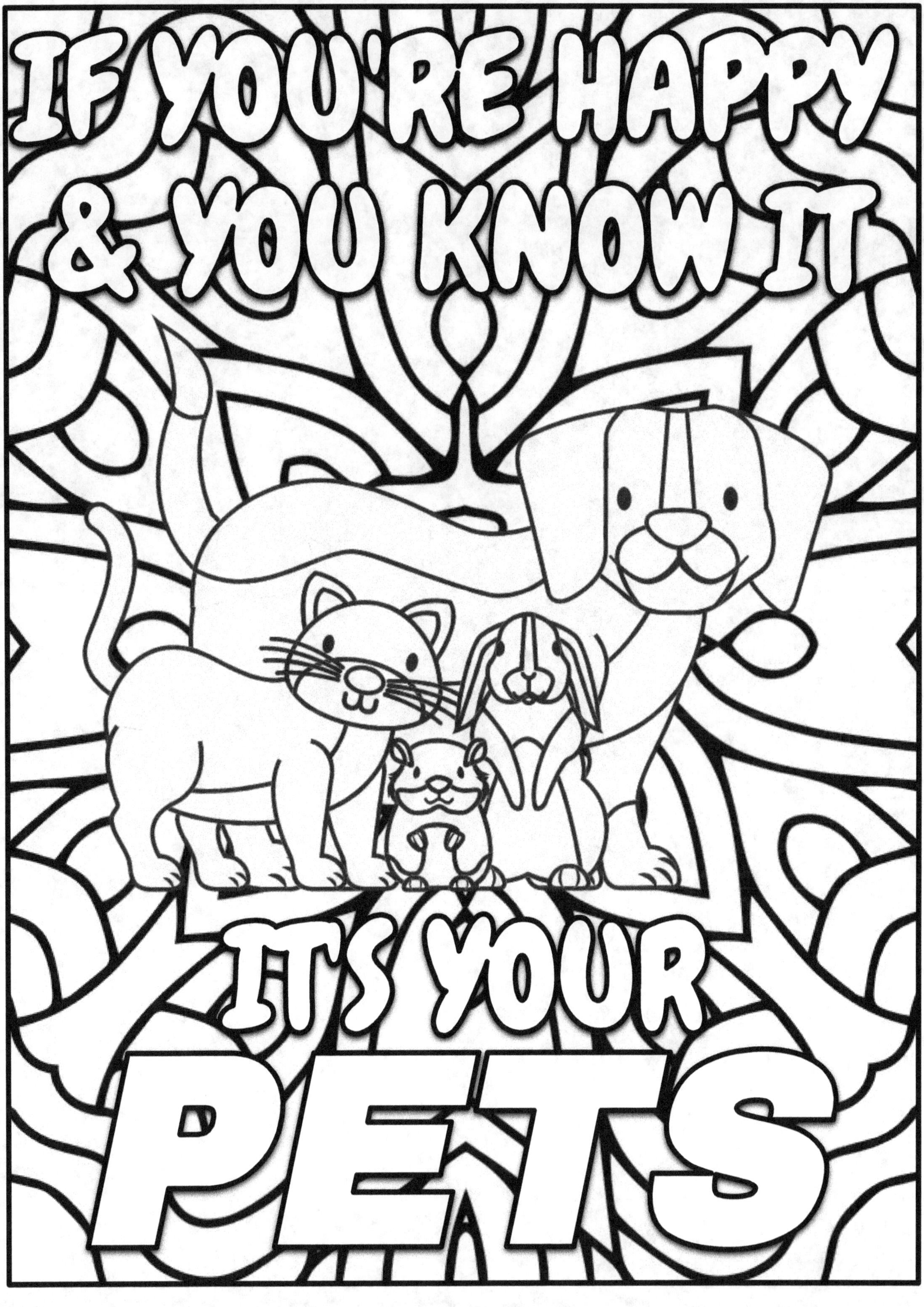
IF YOU'RE HAPPY
& YOU KNOW IT
IT'S YOUR
PETS

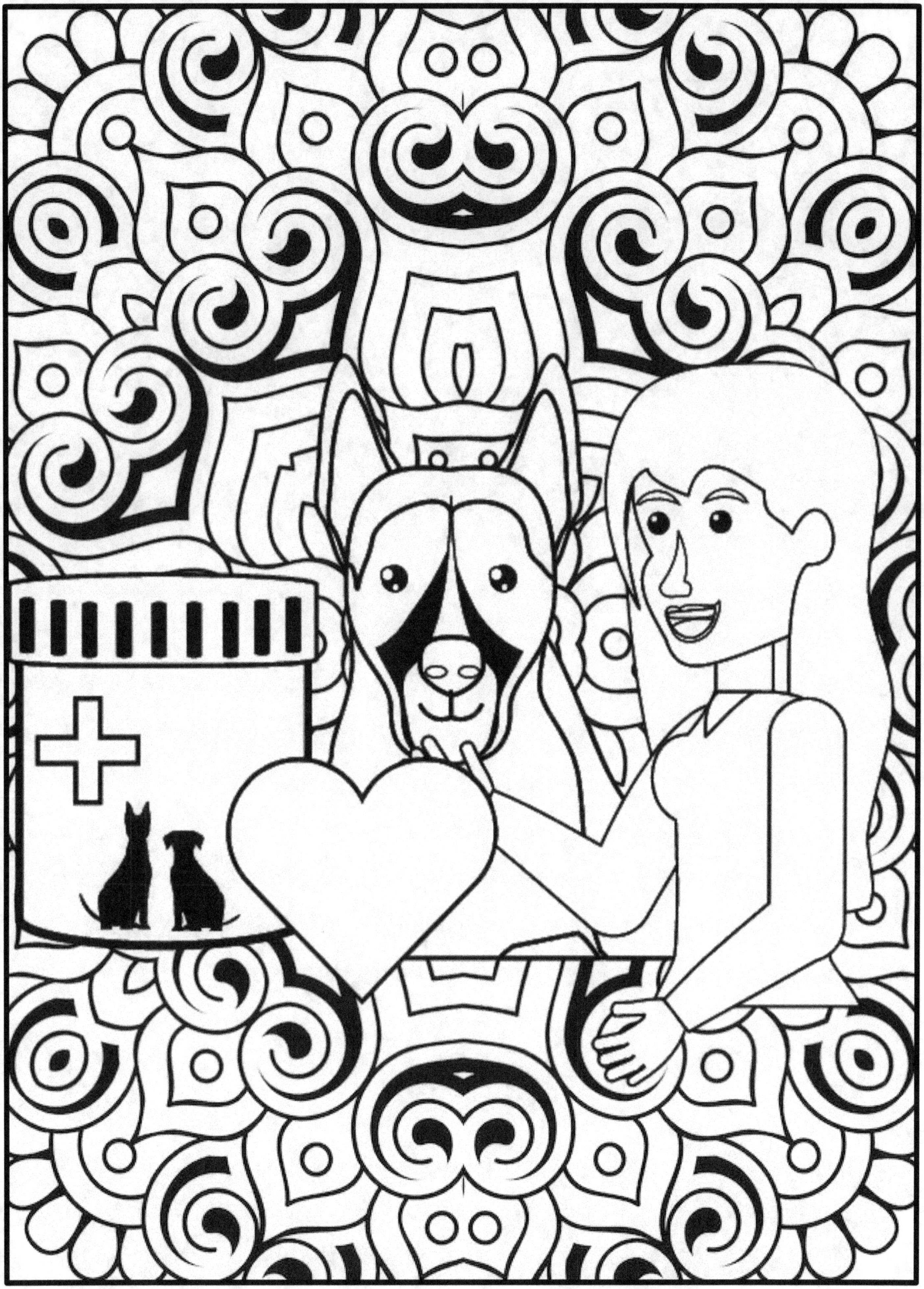

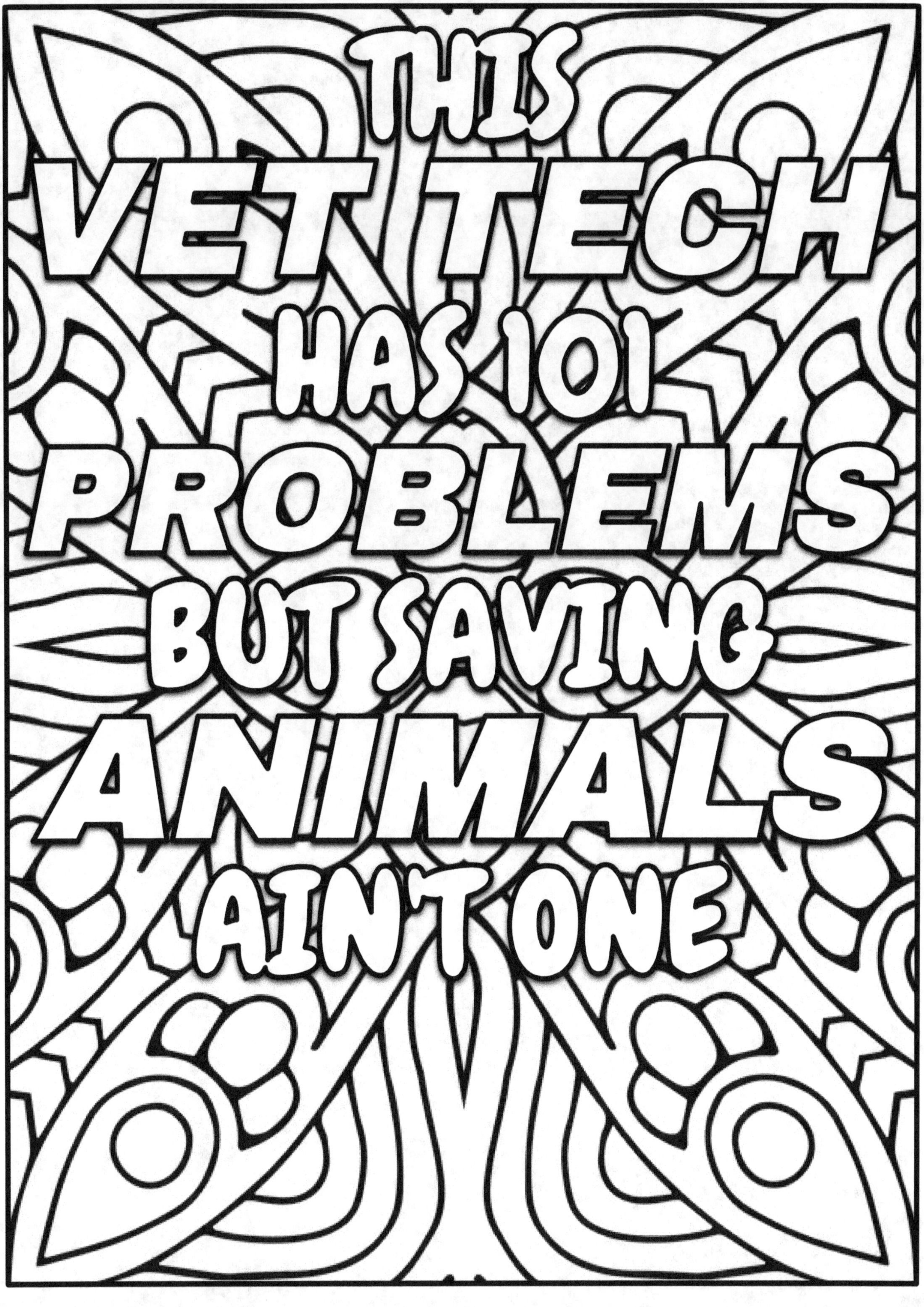
THIS
VET TECH
HAS 101
PROBLEMS
BUT SAVING
ANIMALS
AIN'T ONE

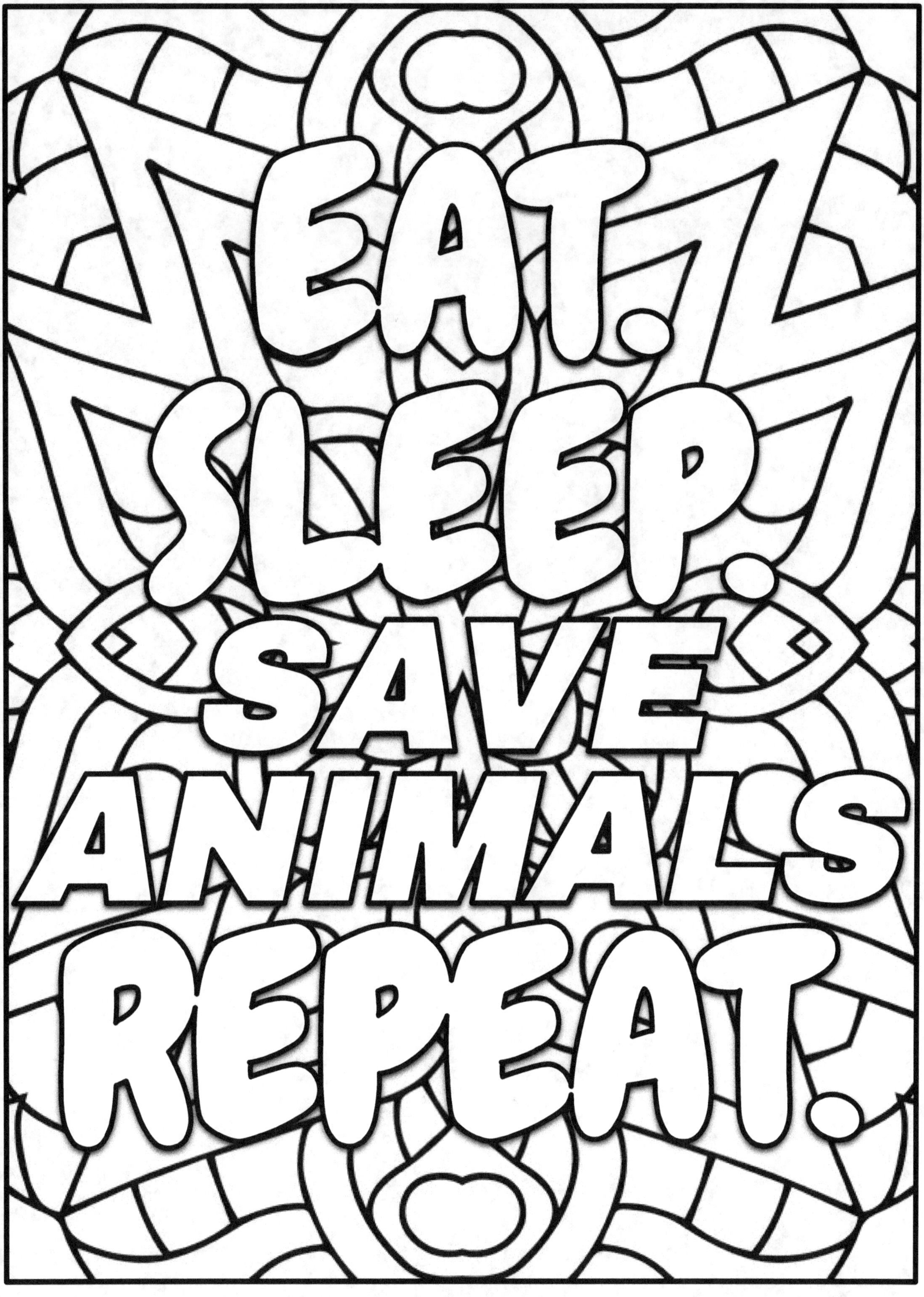
EAT.
SLEEP.
SAVE
ANIMALS
REPEAT.

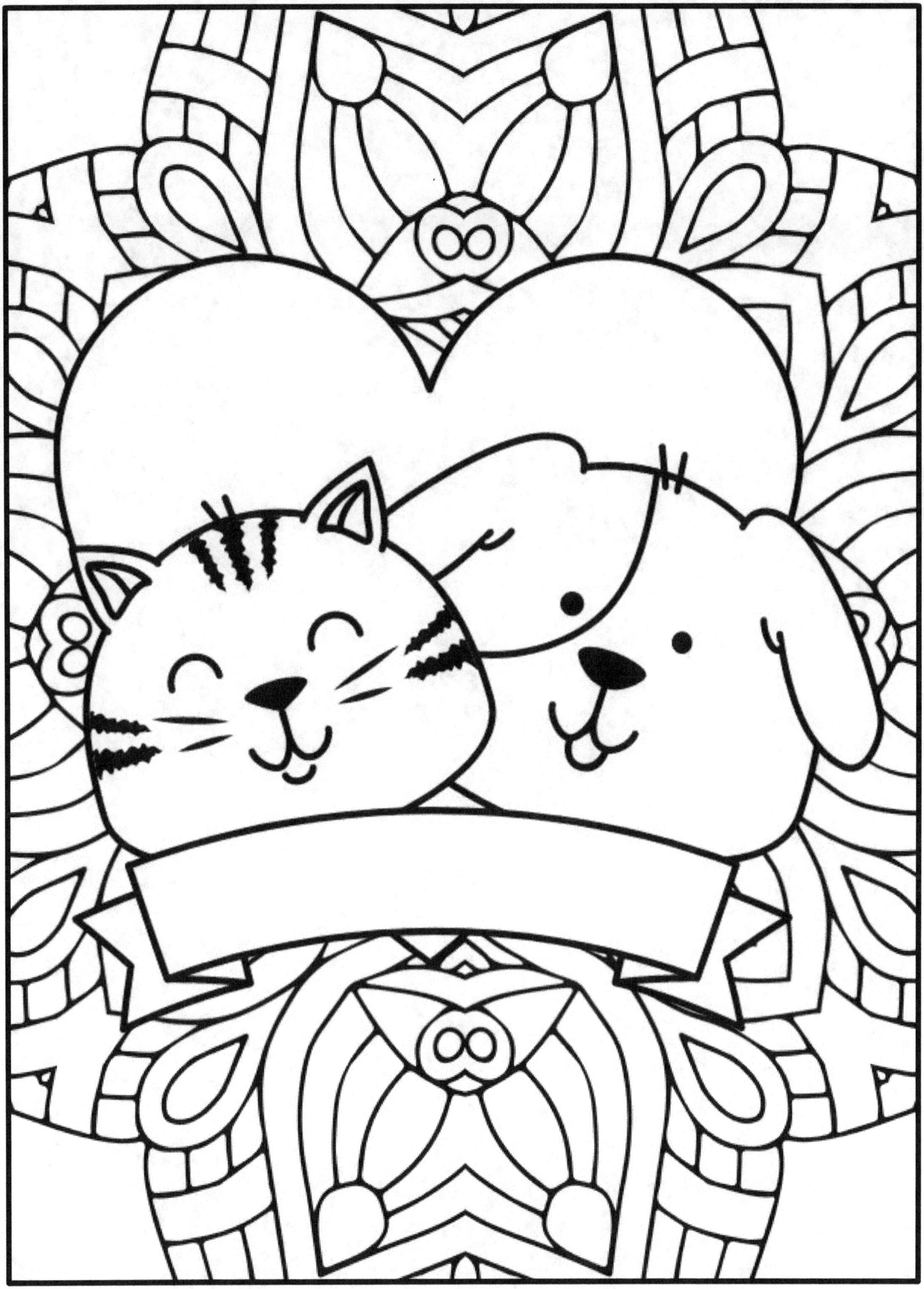

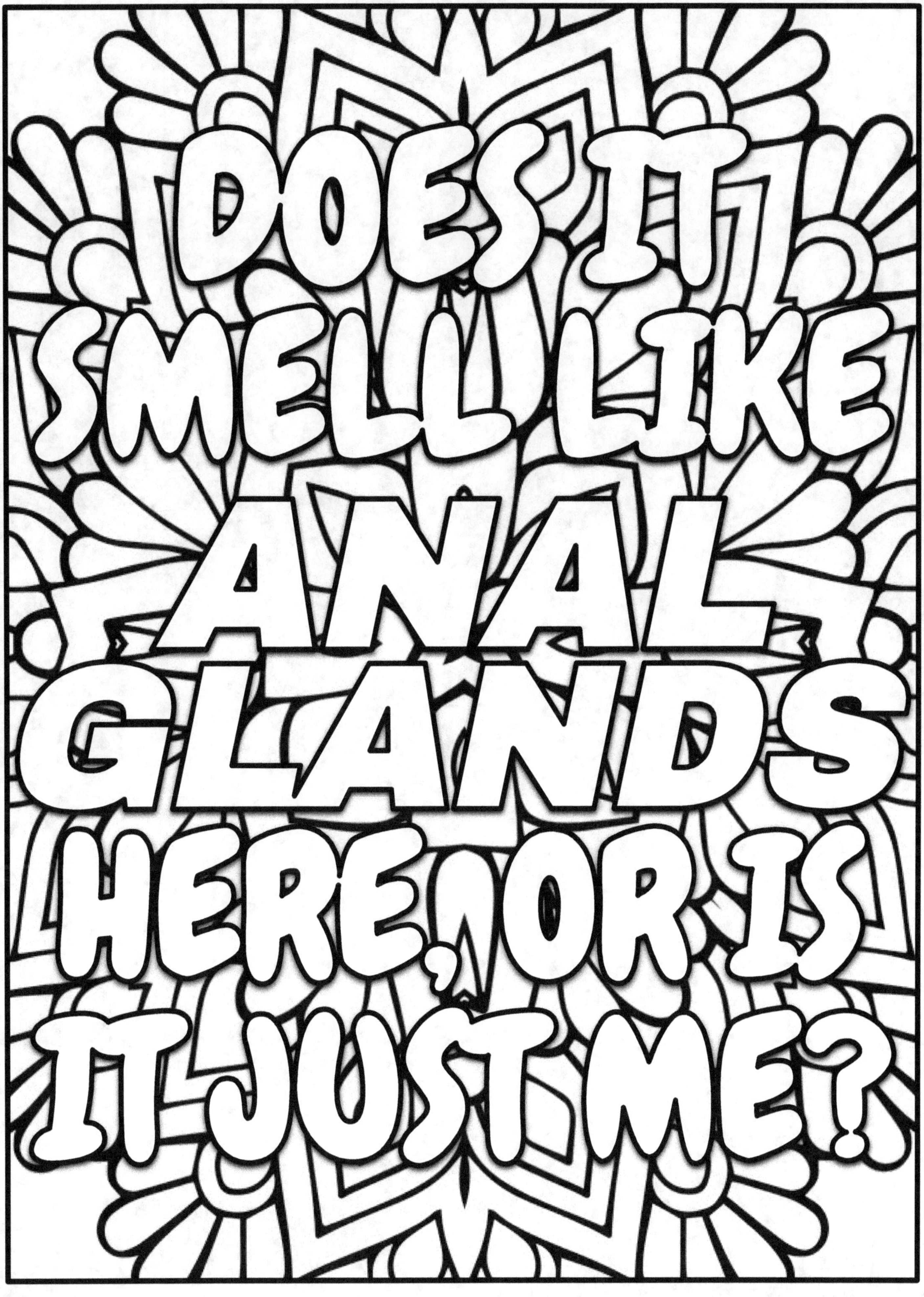
DOES IT
SMELL LIKE
ANAL
GLANDS
HERE, OR IS
IT JUST ME?

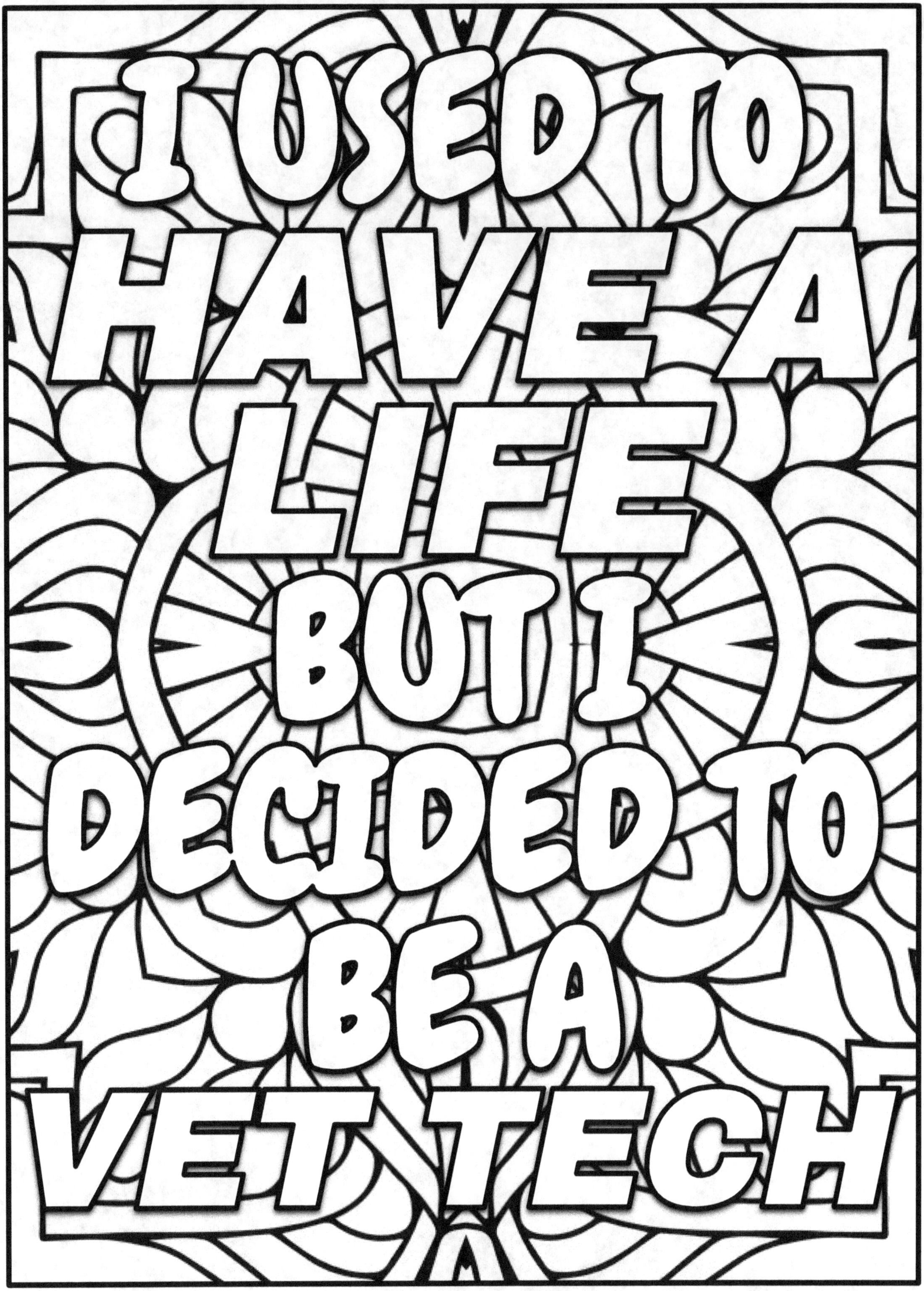
I USED TO
HAVE A
LIFE
BUT I
DECIDED TO
BE A
VET TECH

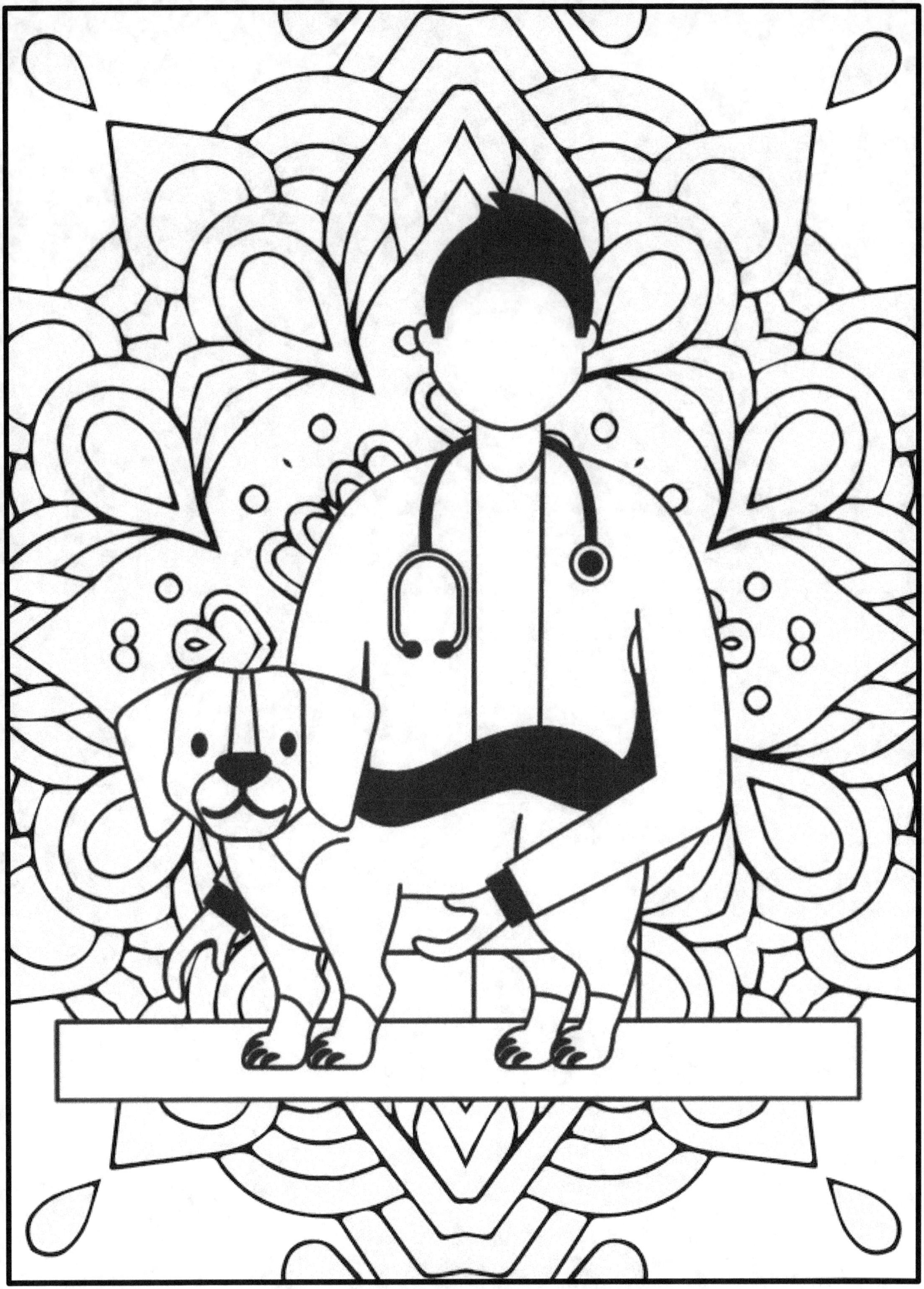

BEING A
VET
TECH
IS EASY
SAID NO
VET TECH EVER

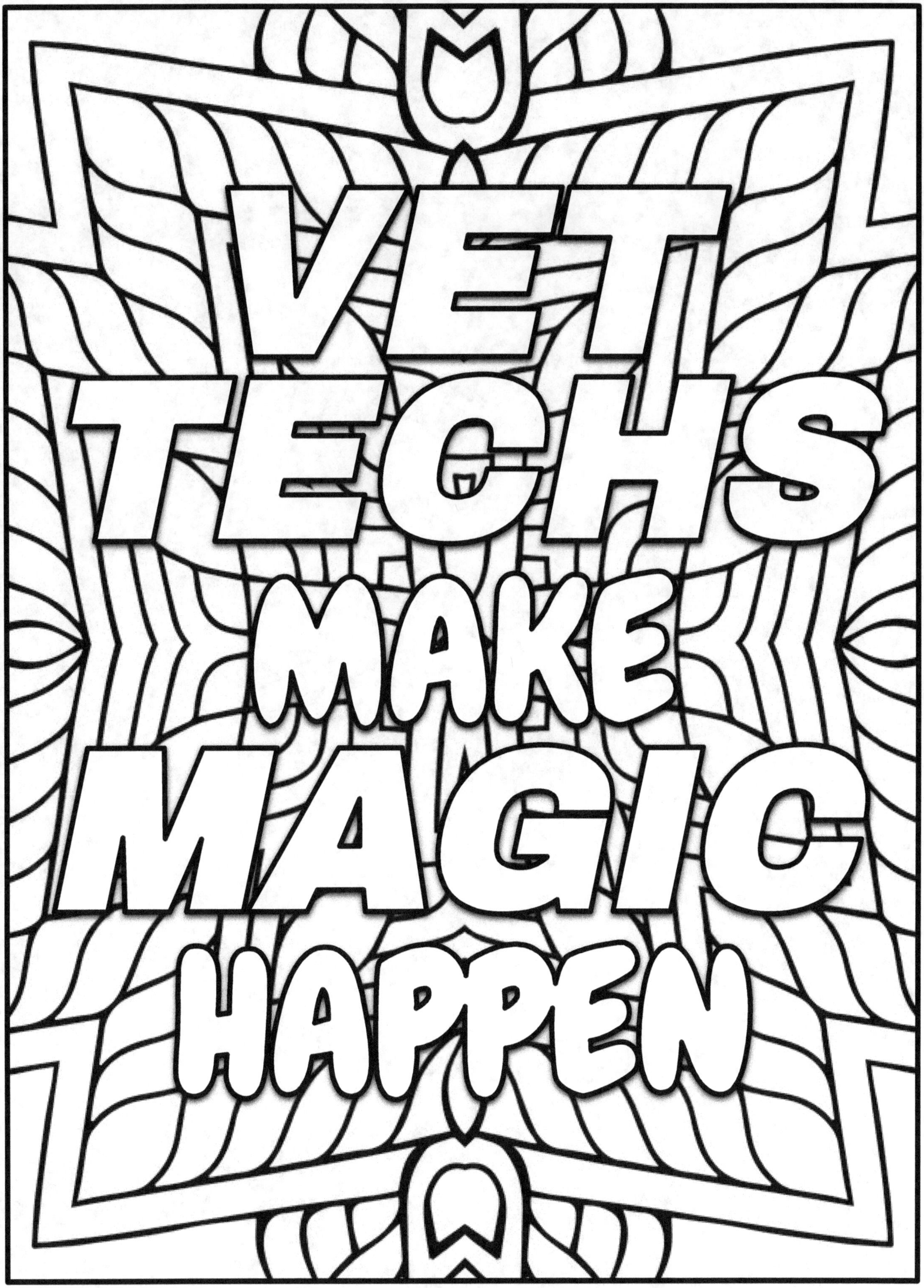
VET
TECHS
MAKE
MAGIC
HAPPEN

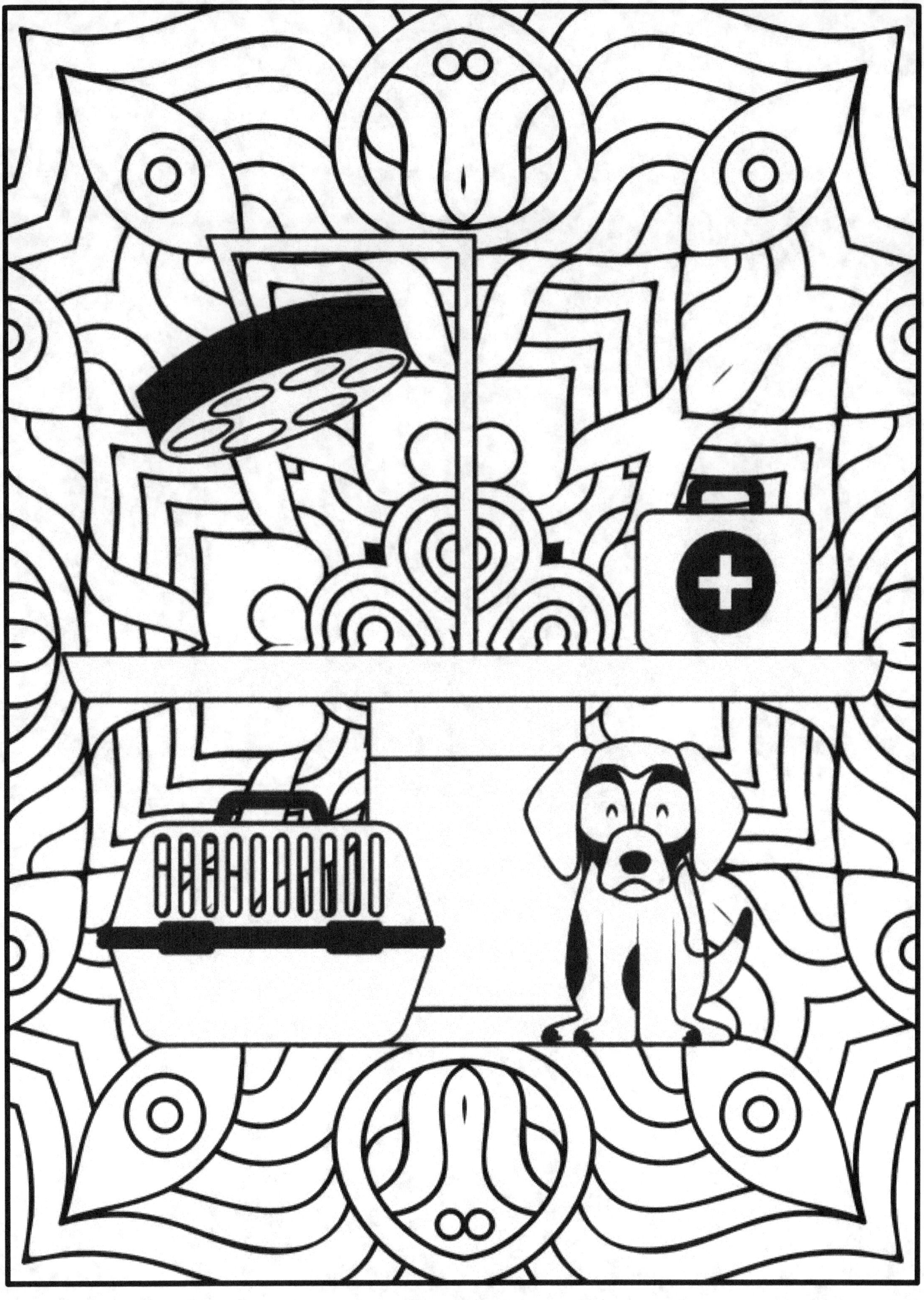

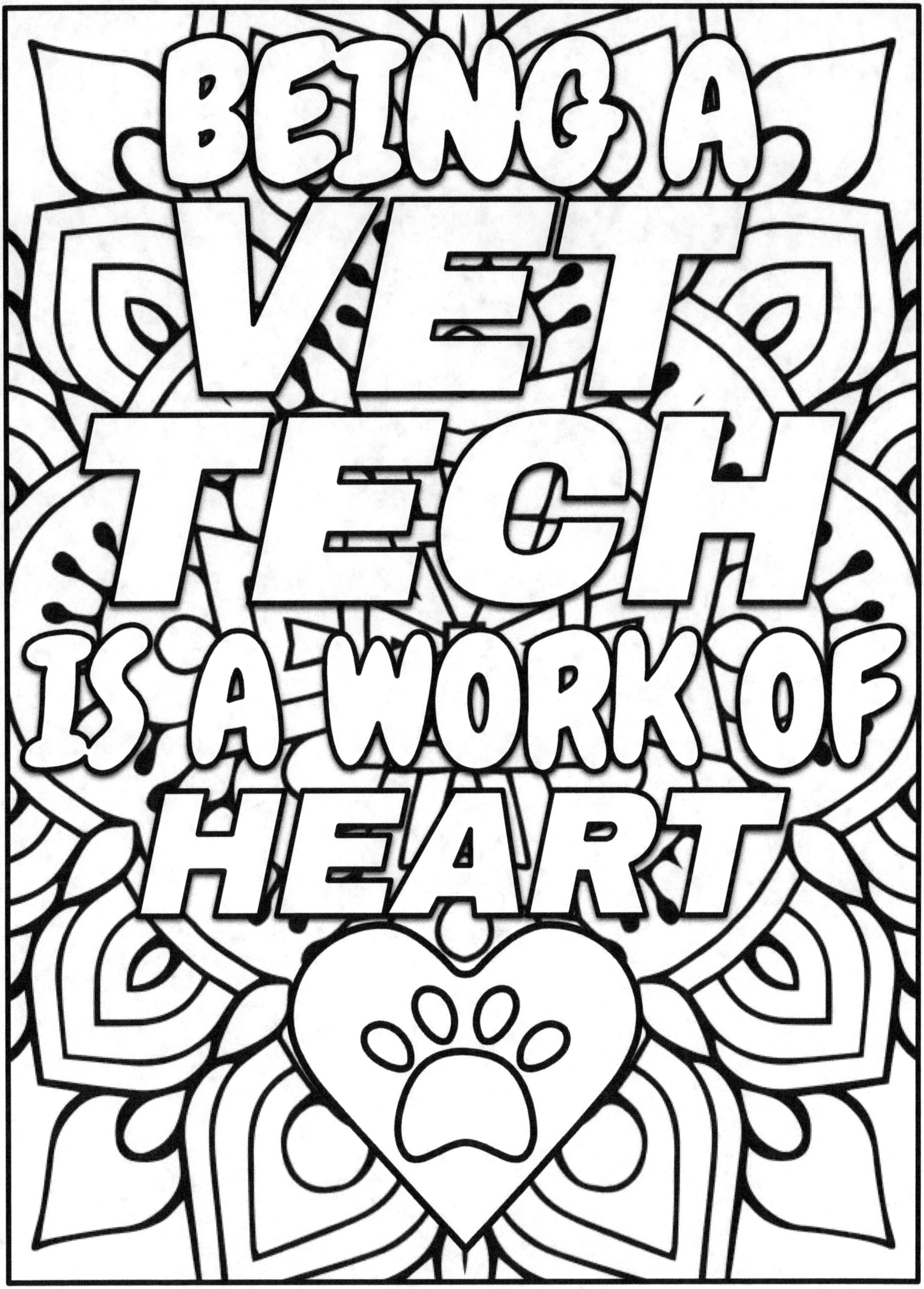
BEING A
VET
TECH
IS A WORK OF
HEART

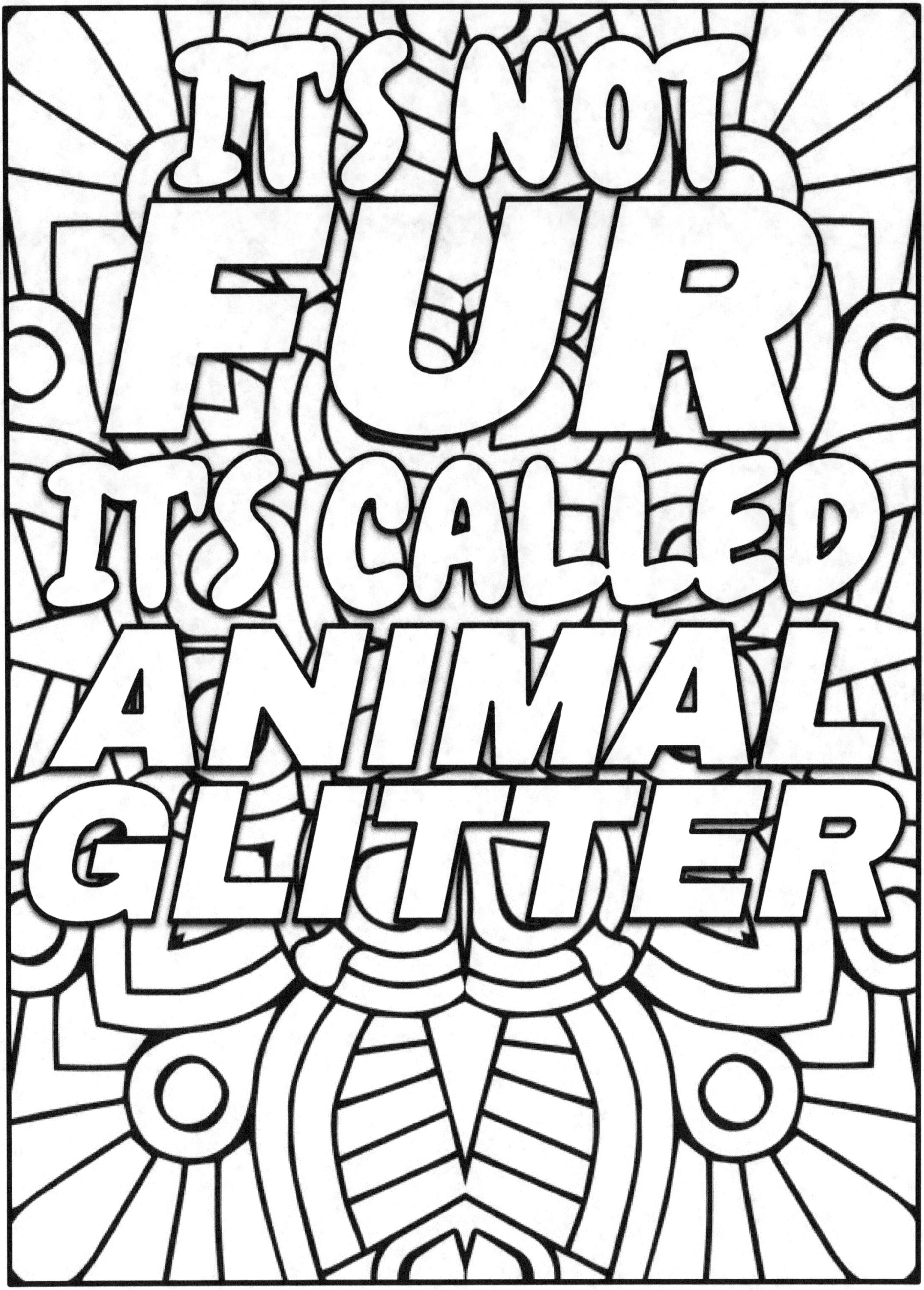
ITS NOT
FUR
ITS CALLED
ANIMAL
GLITTER

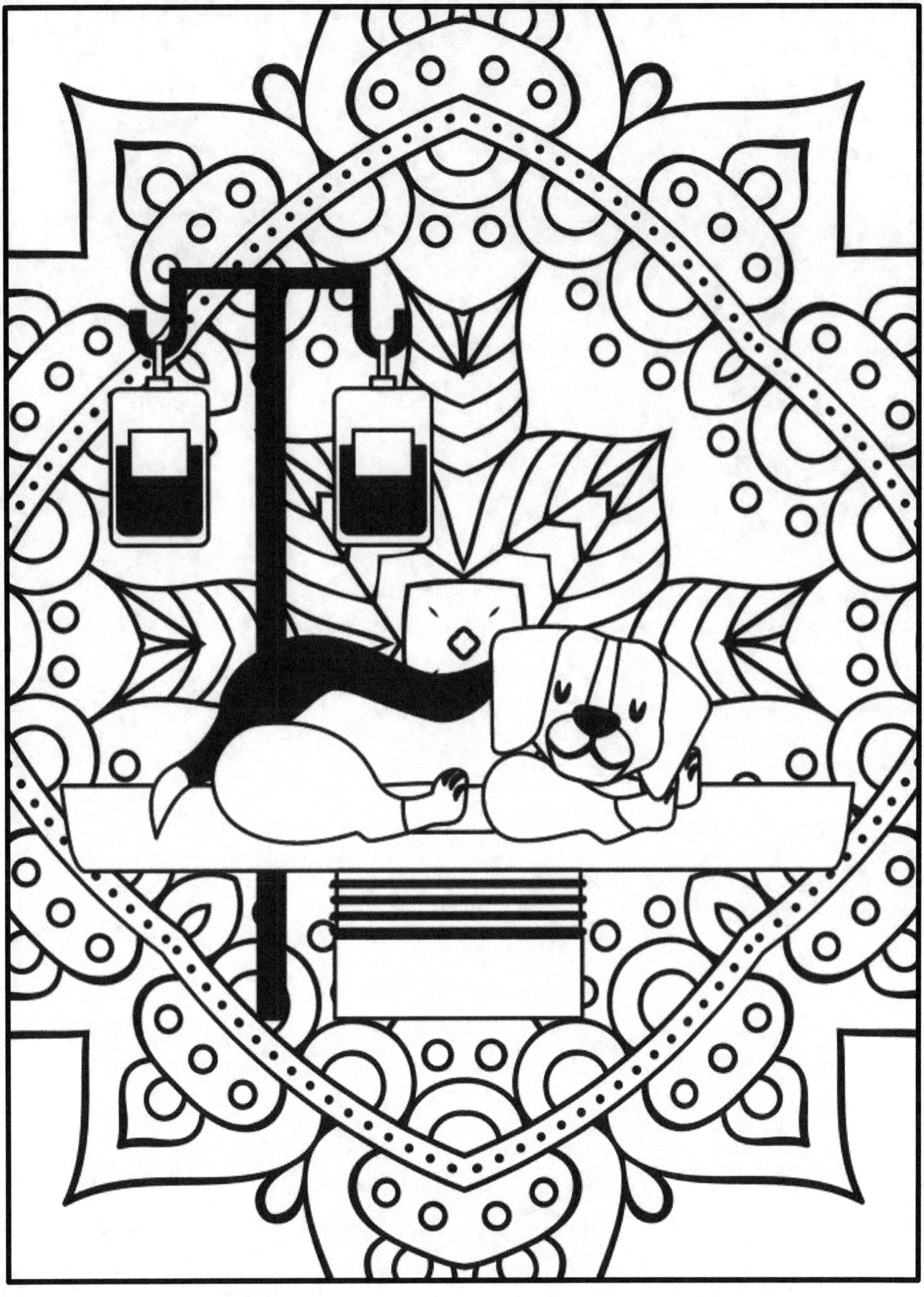

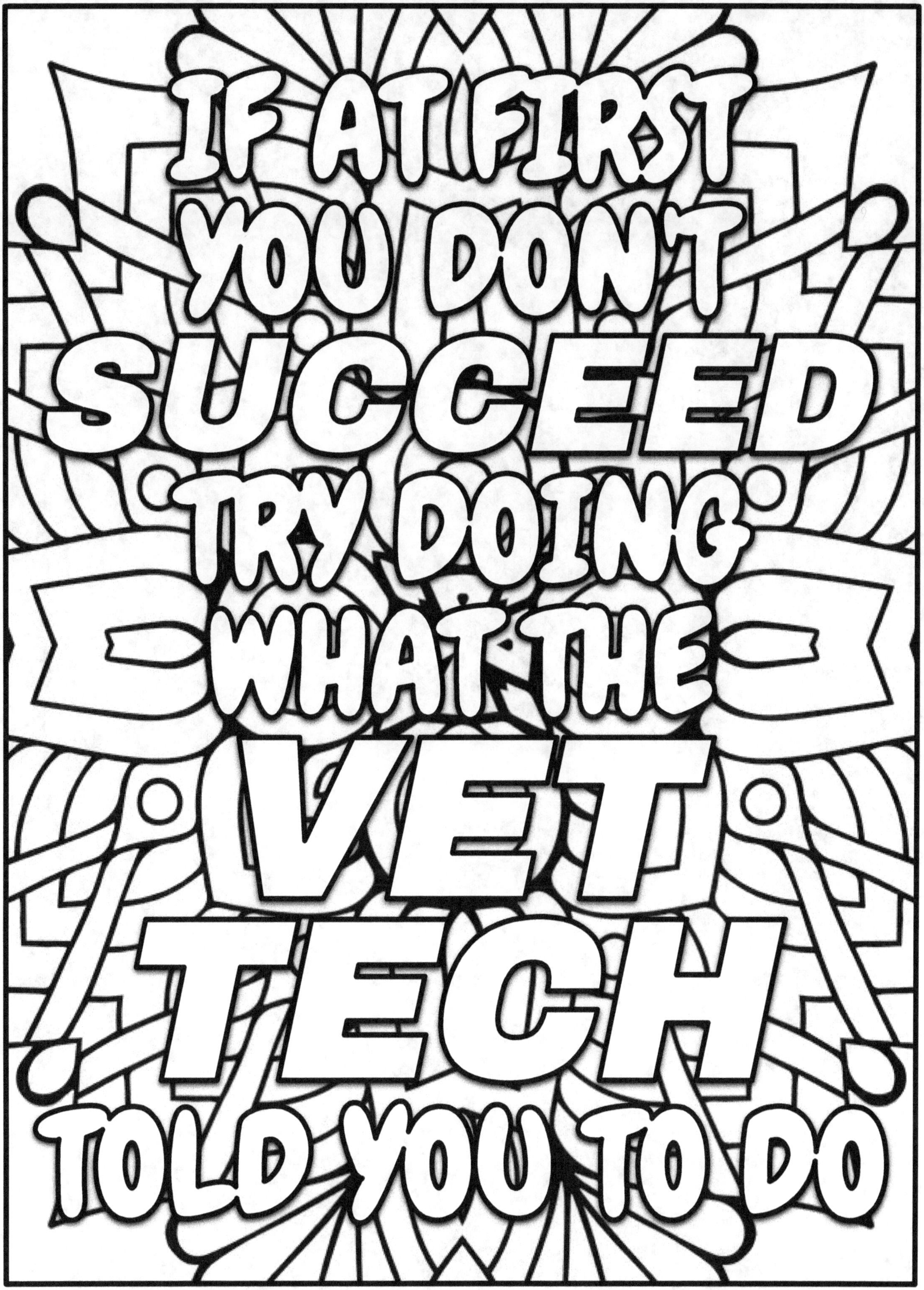
IF AT FIRST
YOU DON'T
SUCCEED
TRY DOING
WHAT THE
VET
TECH
TOLD YOU TO DO

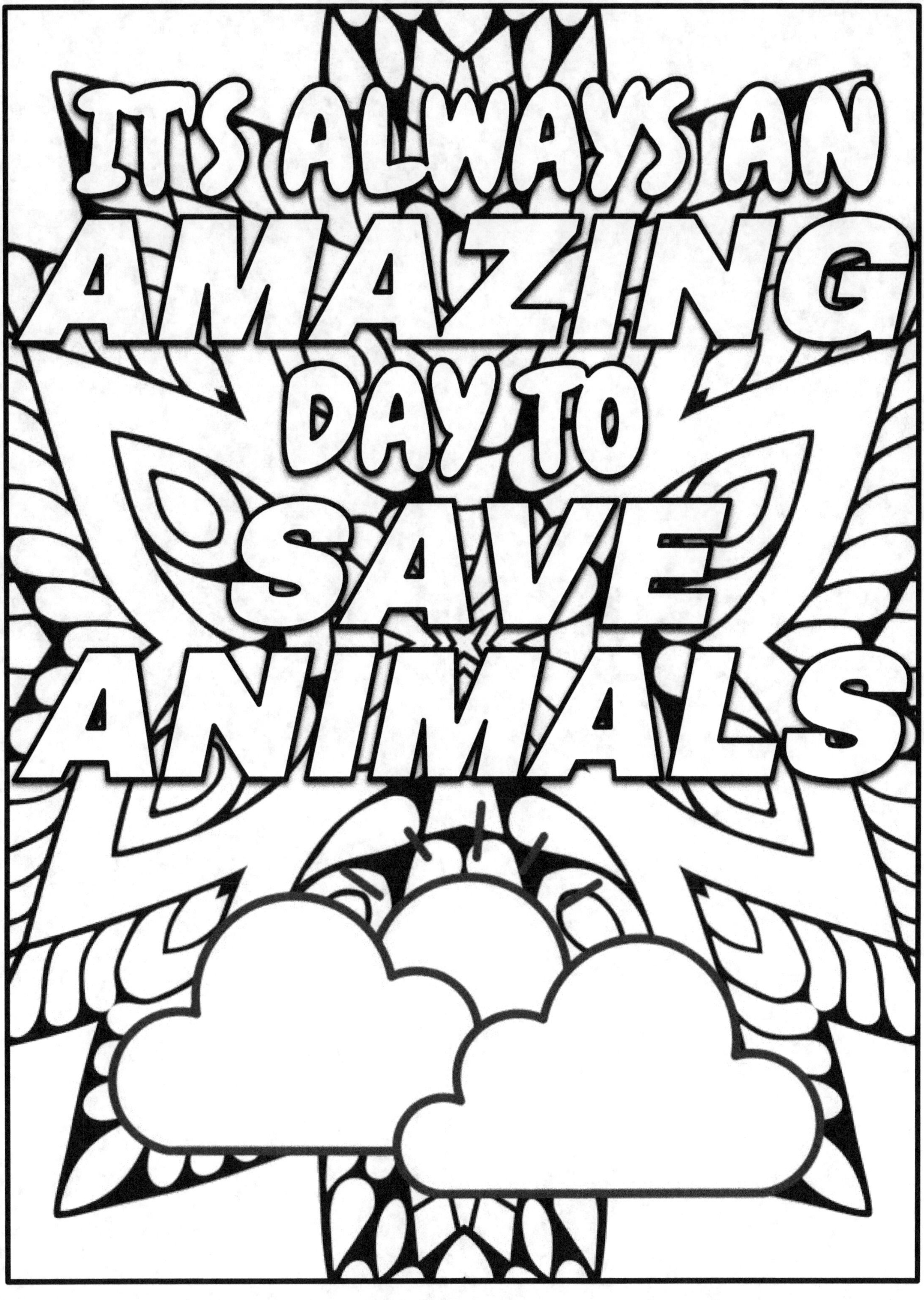
IT'S ALWAYS AN
AMAZING
DAY TO
SAVE ANIMALS

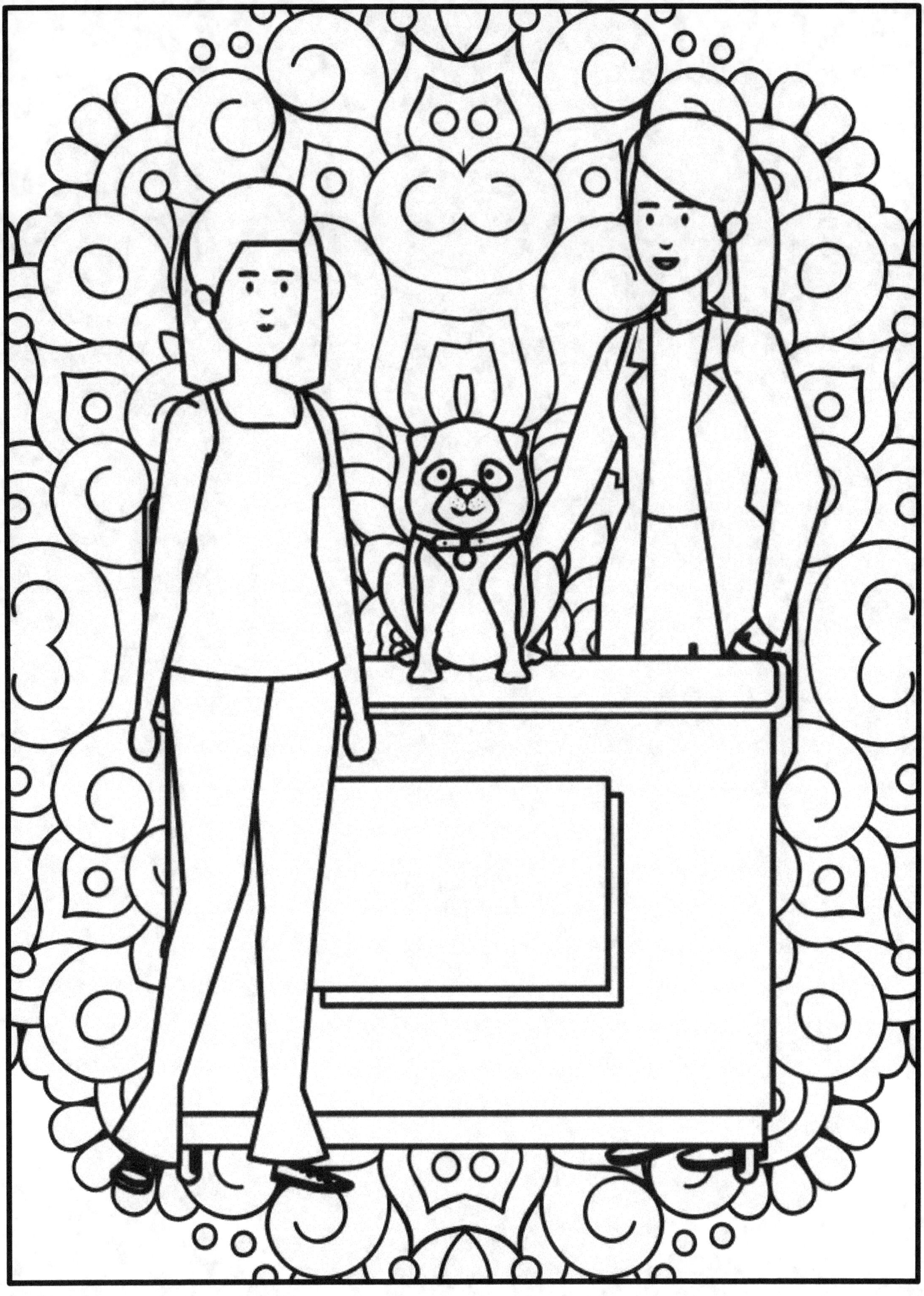

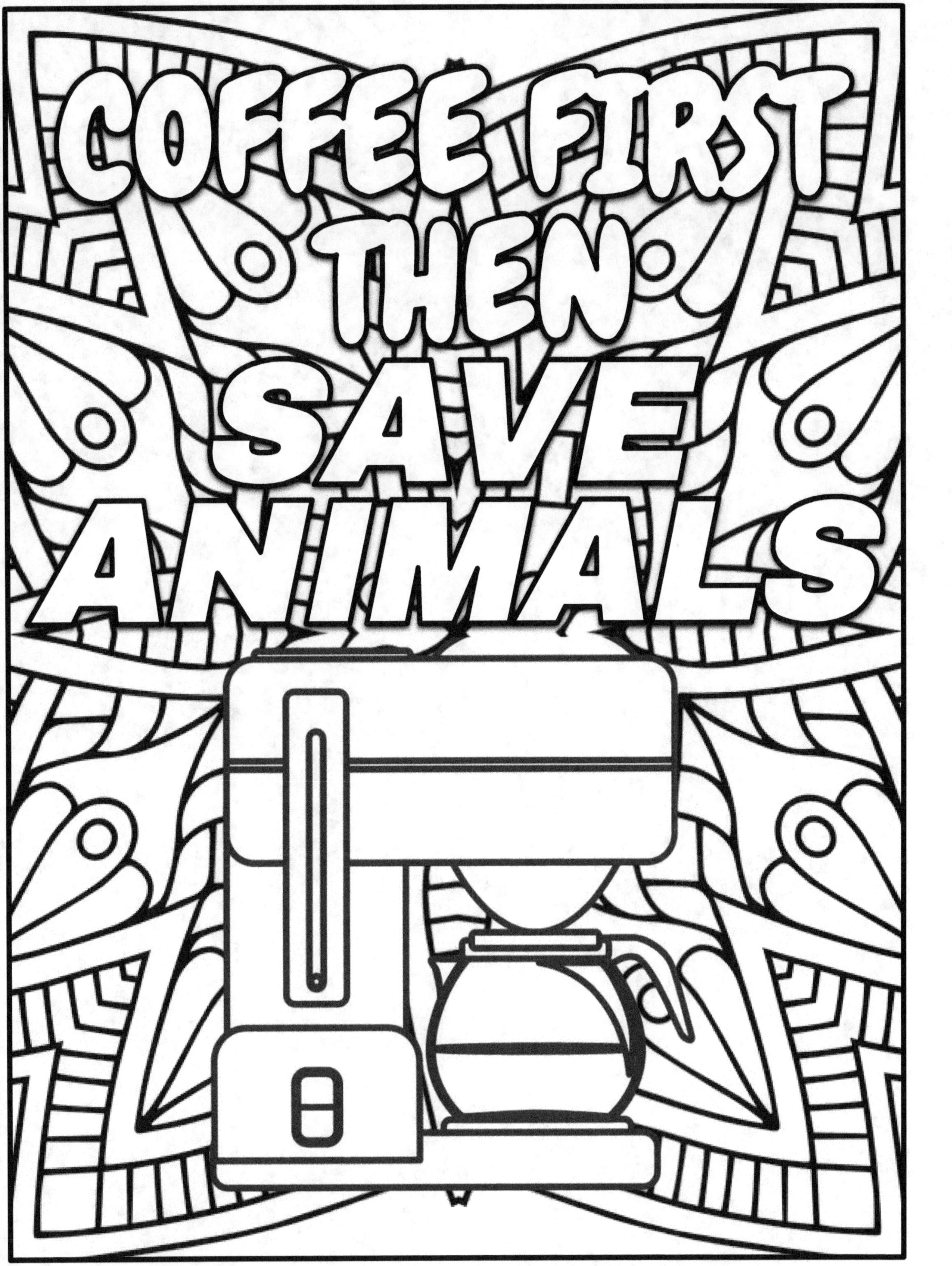
COFFEE FIRST
THEN
SAVE
ANIMALS

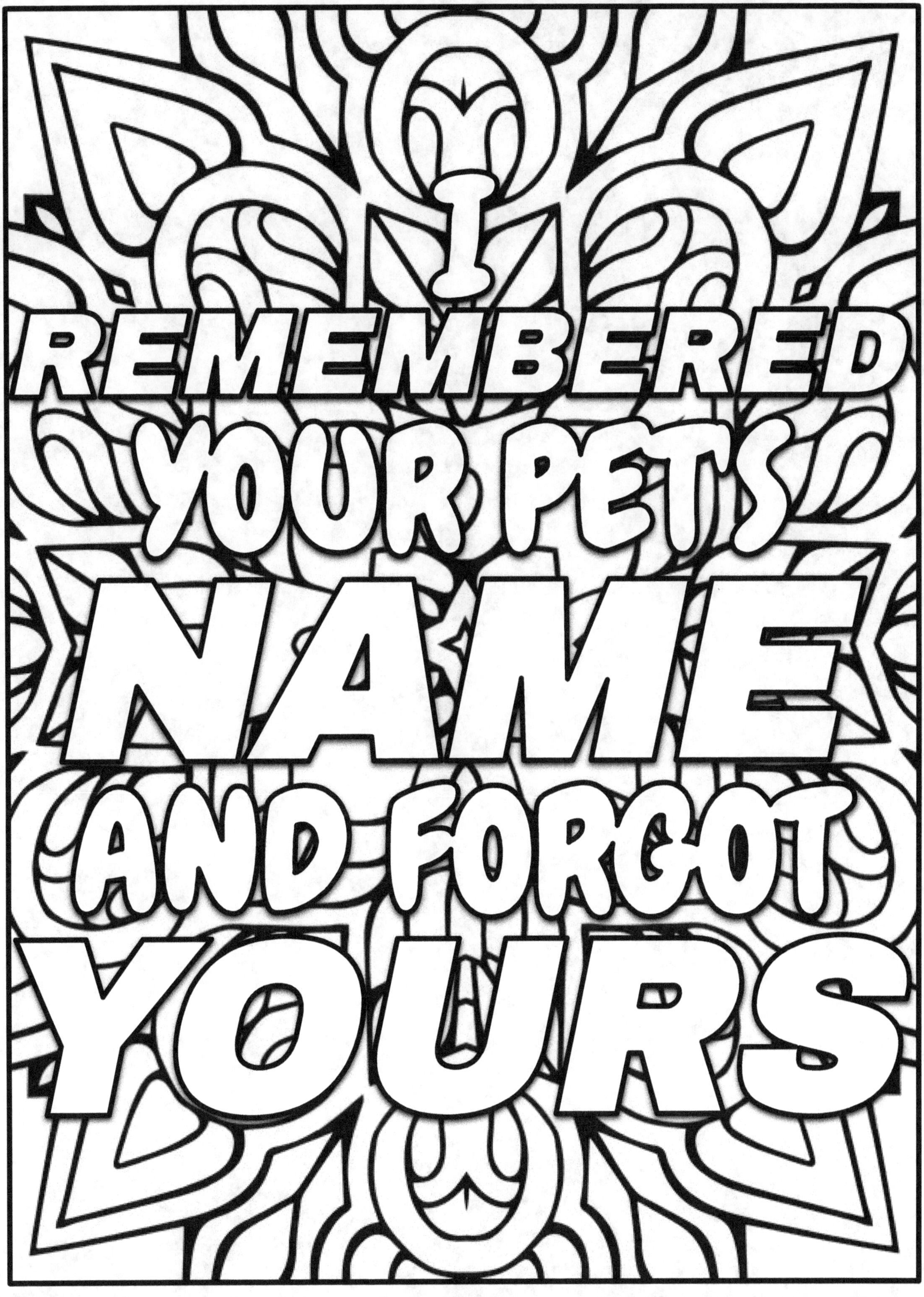
I
REMEMBERED
YOUR PET'S
NAME
AND FORGOT
YOURS

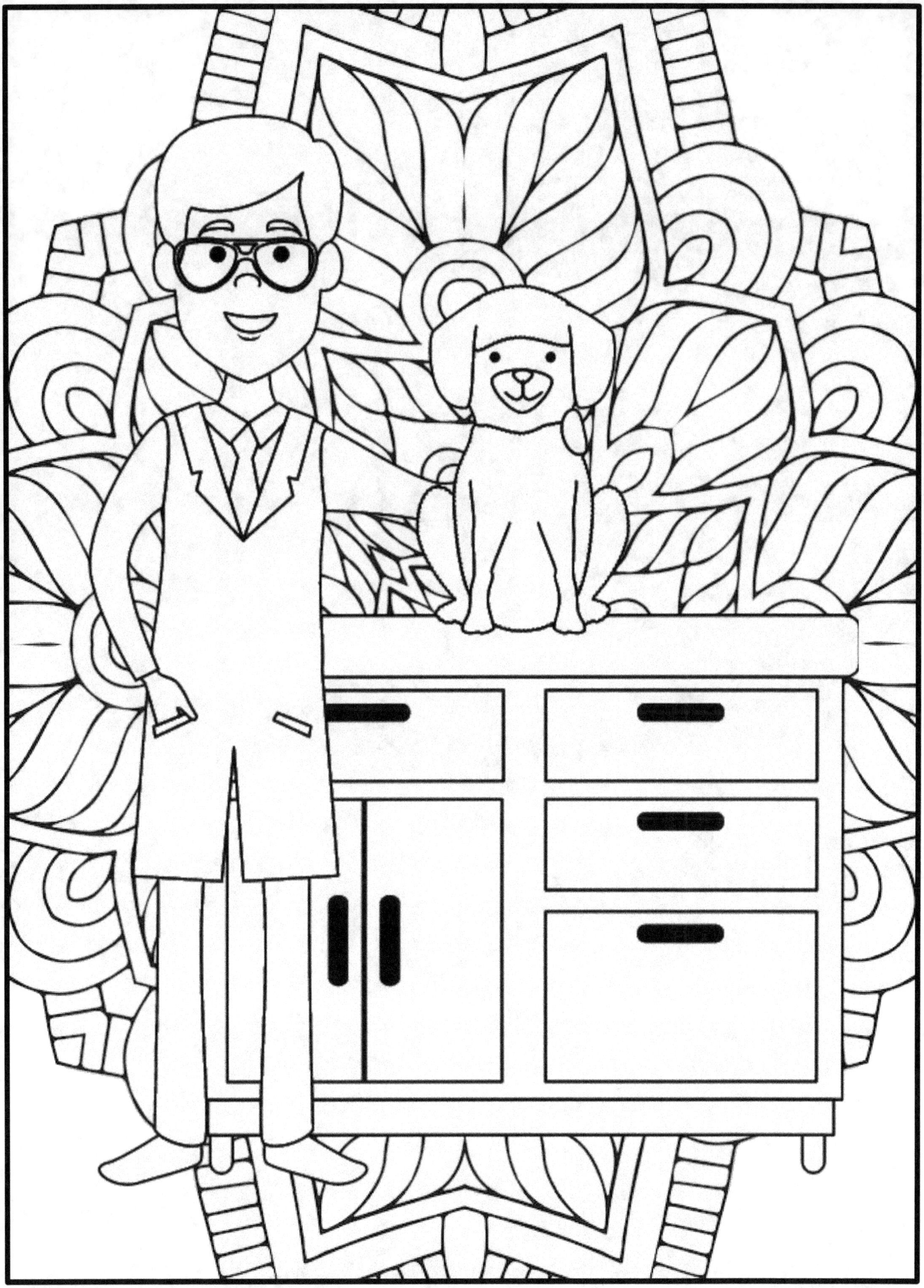

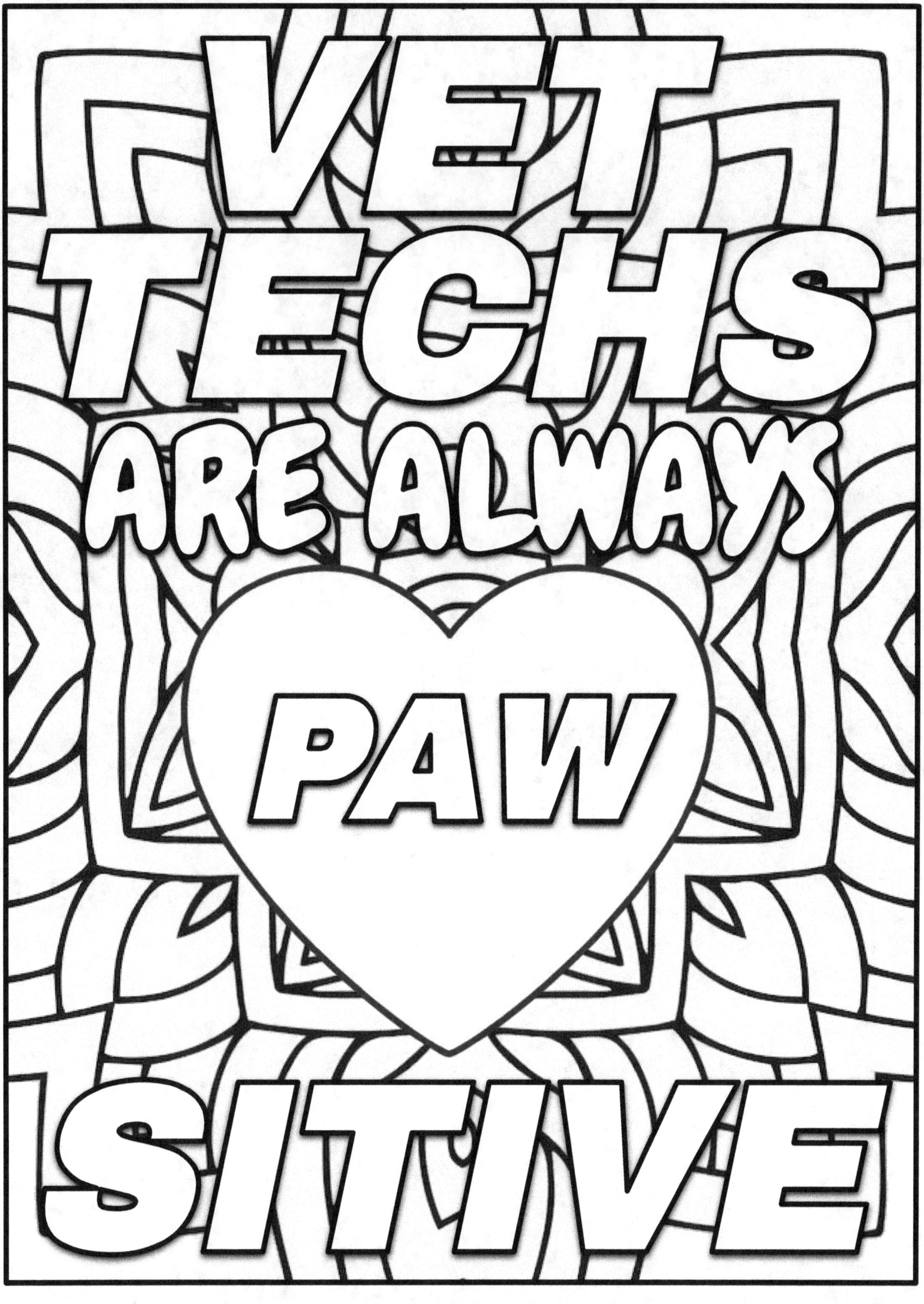
VET
TECHS
ARE ALWAYS
PAW
SITIVE

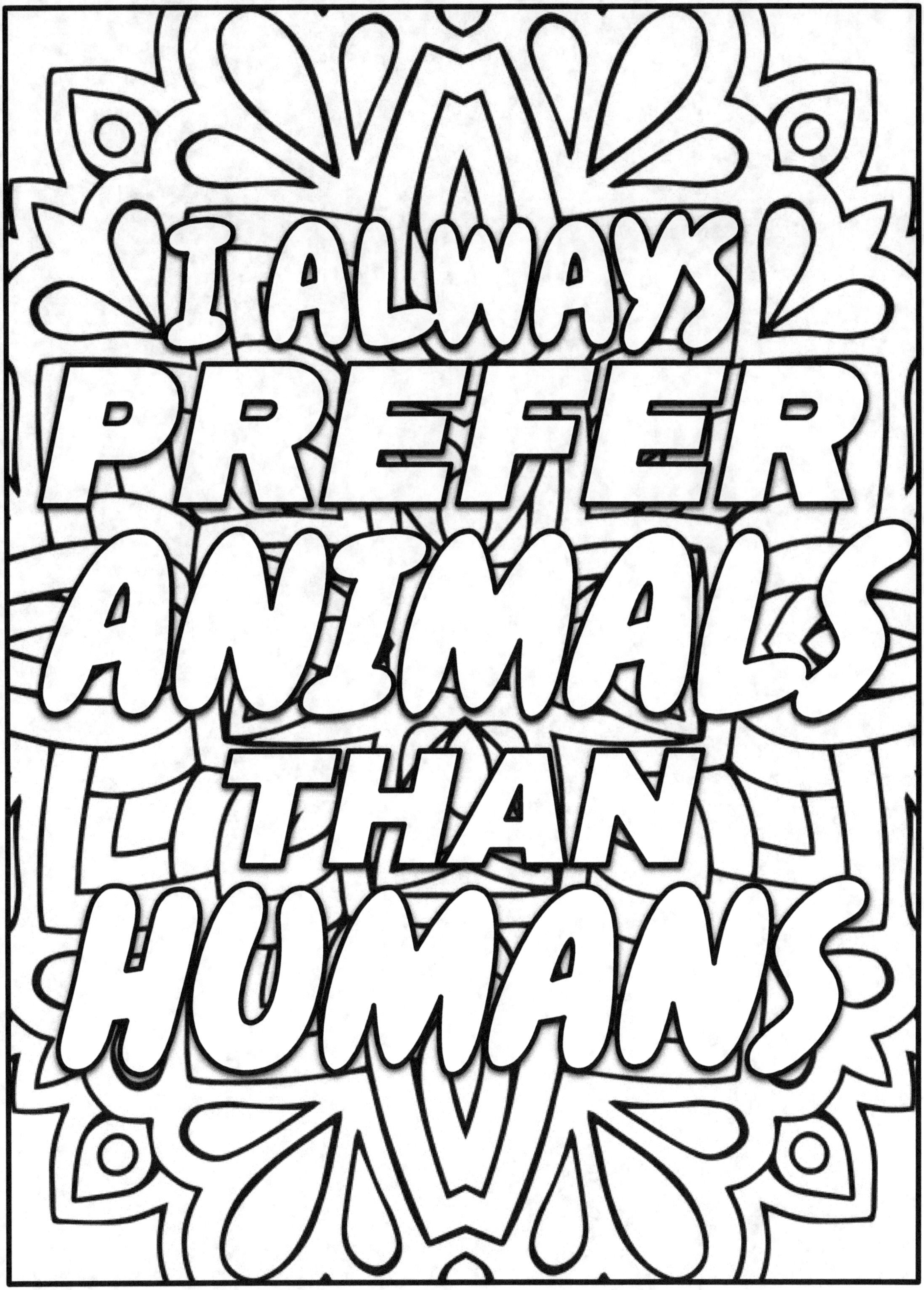
I ALWAYS
PREFER
ANIMALS
THAN
HUMANS

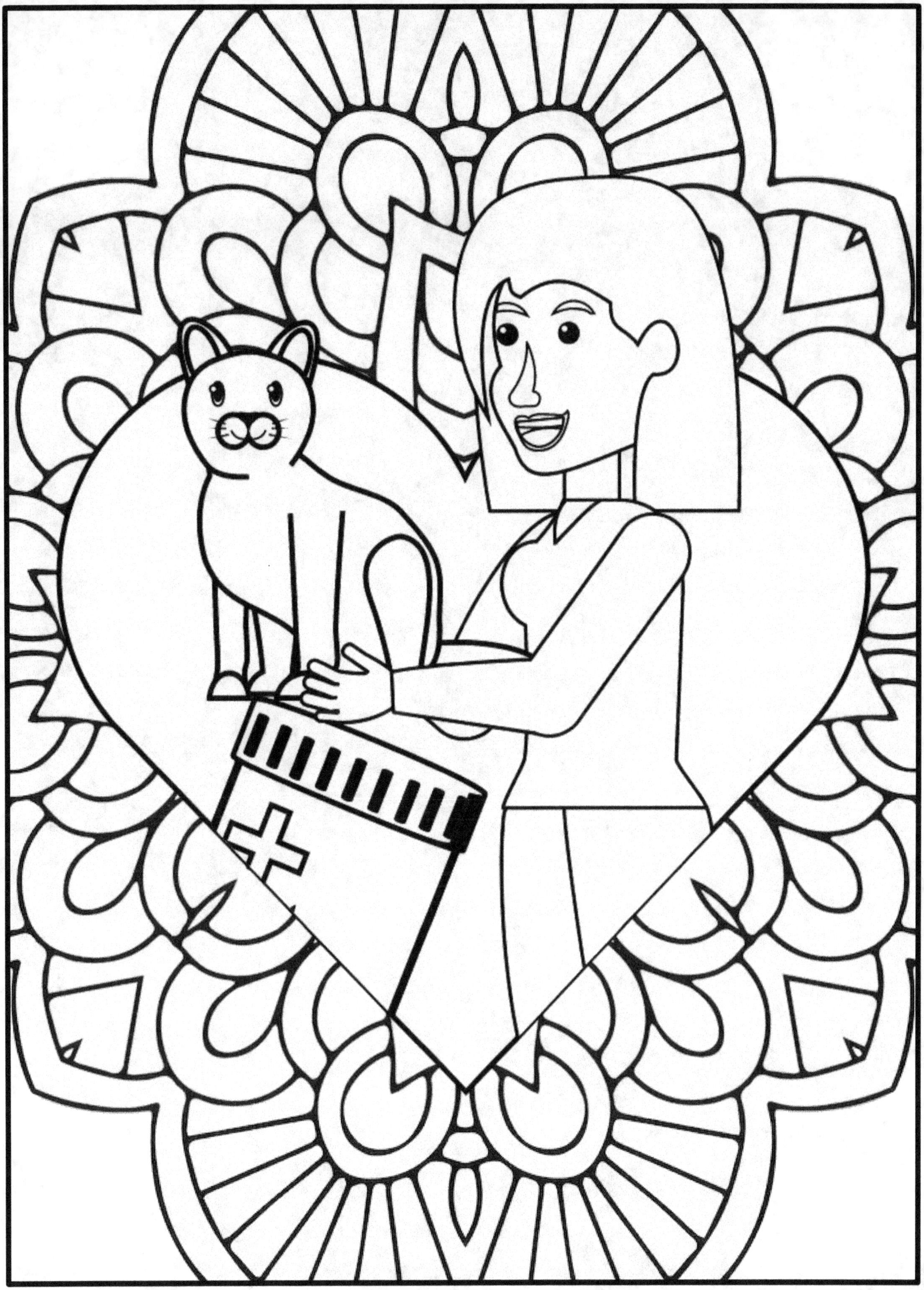

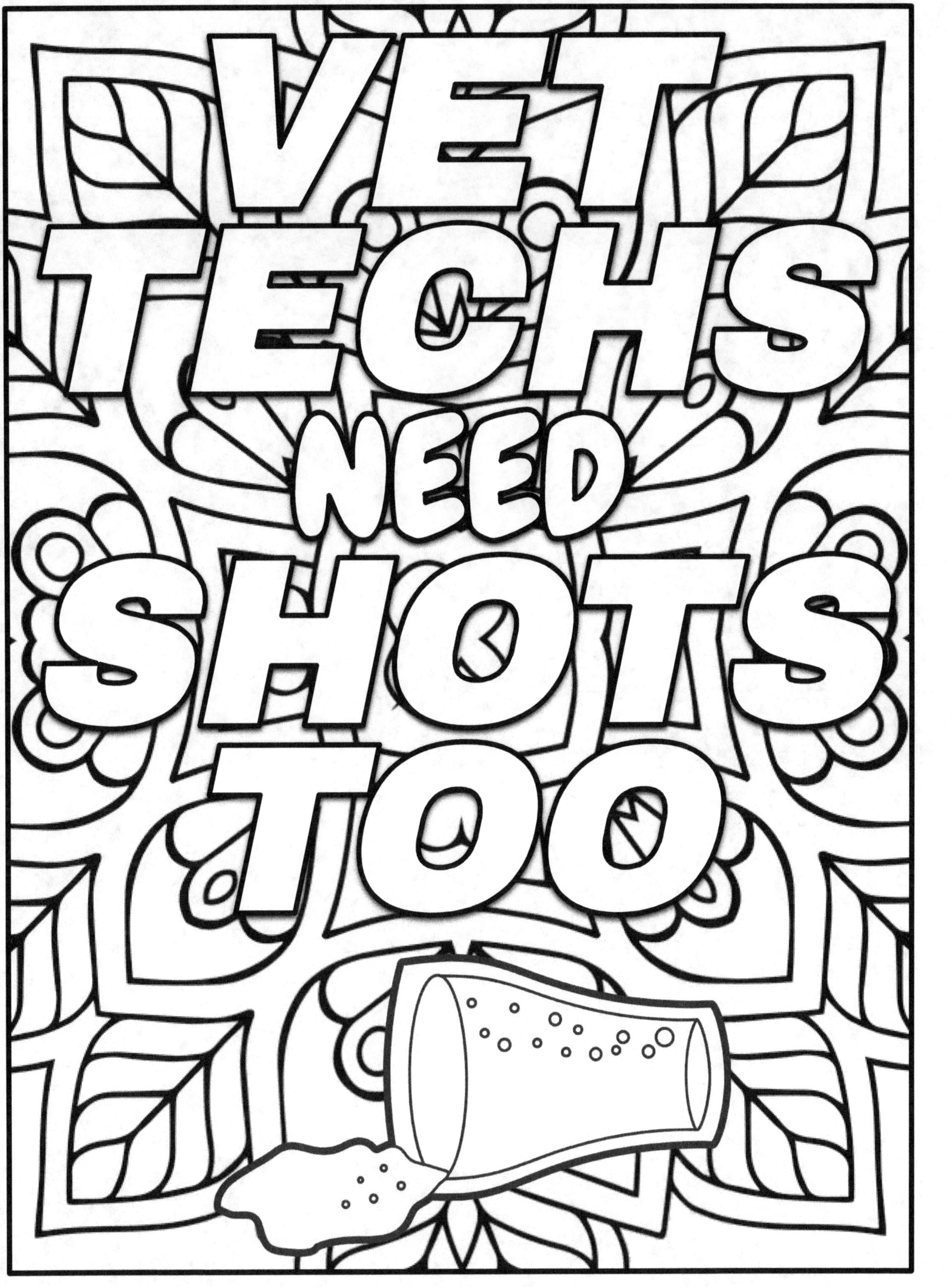
VET
TECHS
NEED
SHOTS
TOO

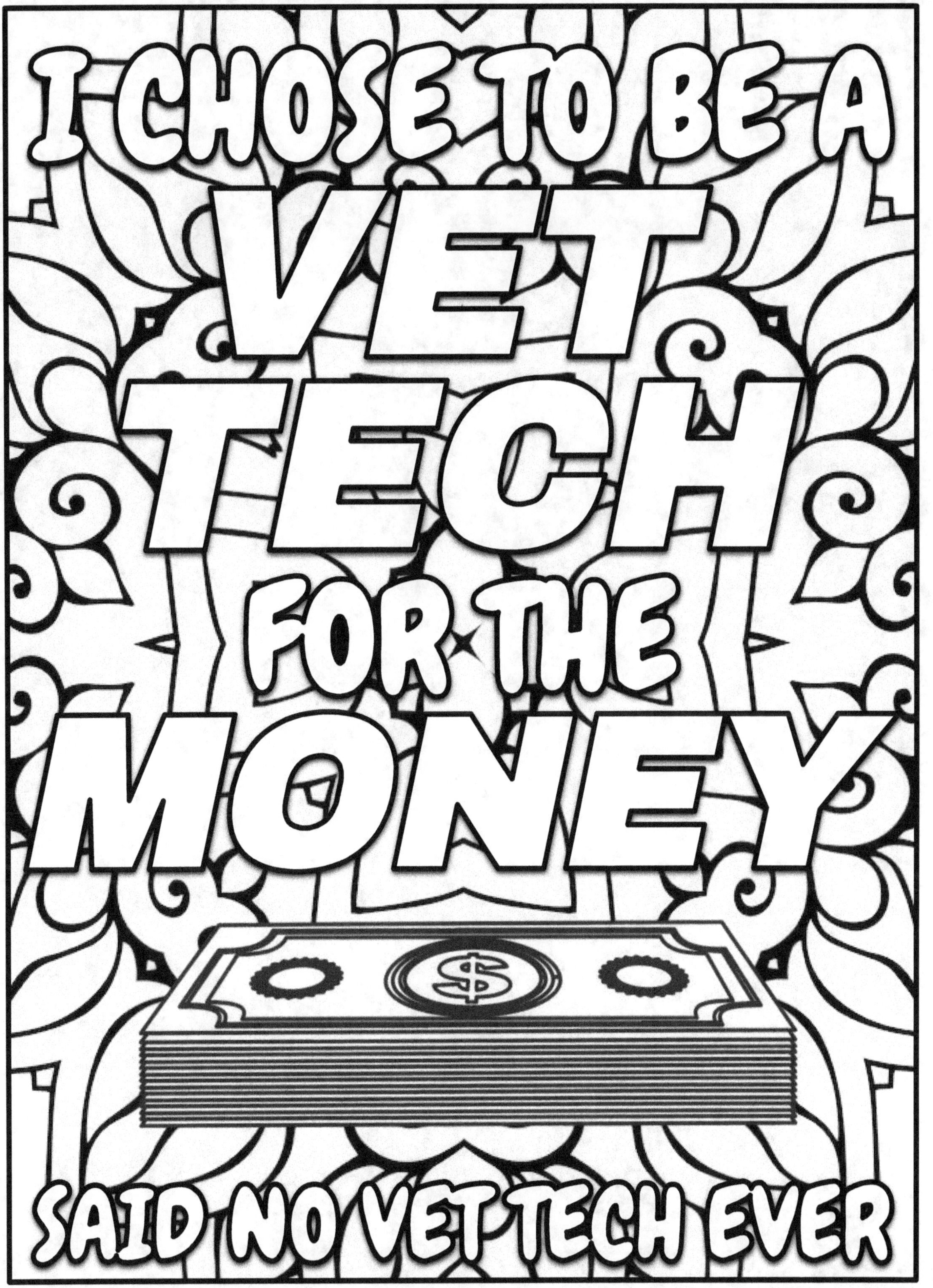
I CHOSE TO BE A
VET
TECH
FOR THE
MONEY
SAID NO VET TECH EVER

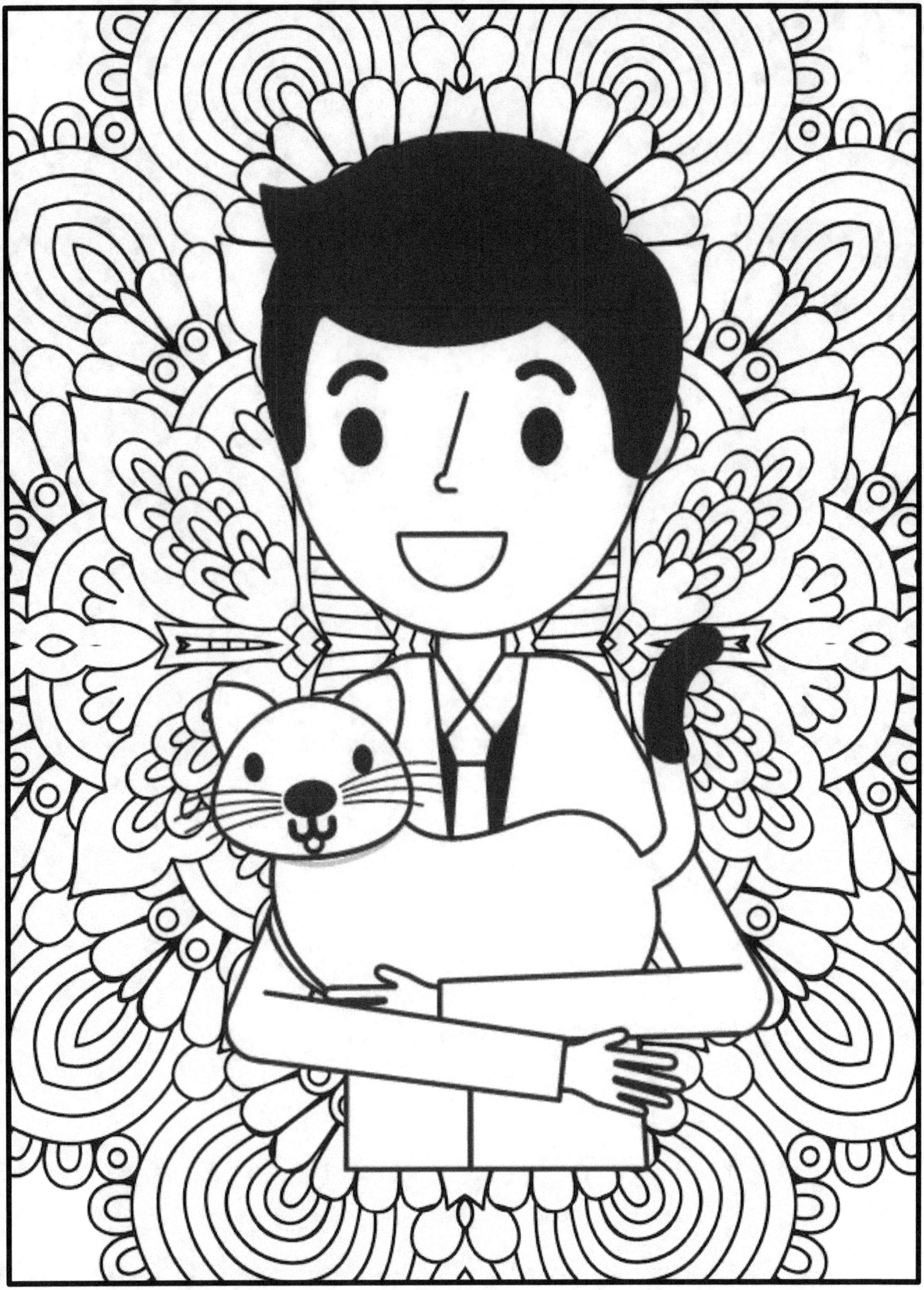

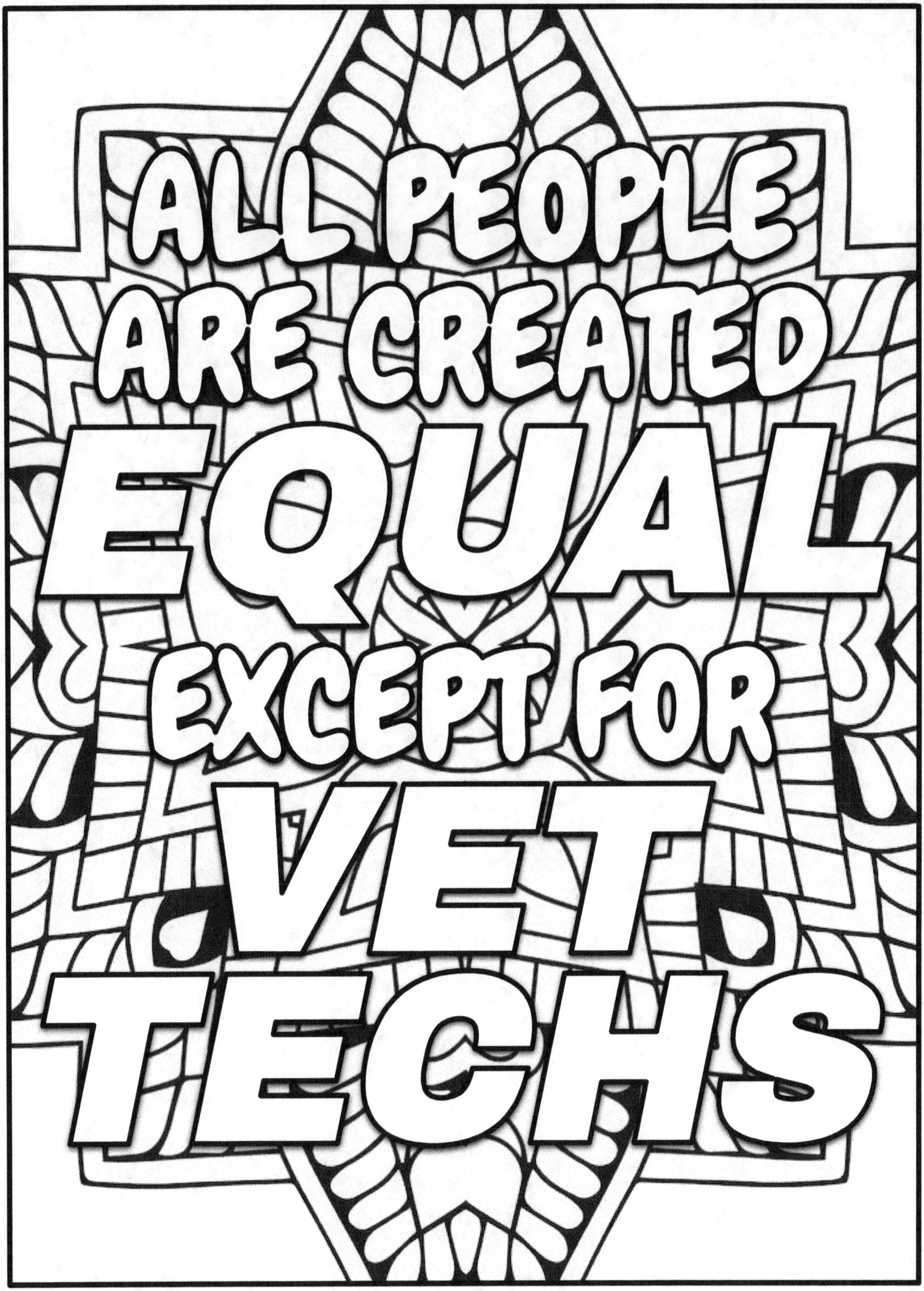
ALL PEOPLE
ARE CREATED
EQUAL
EXCEPT FOR
VET
TECHS

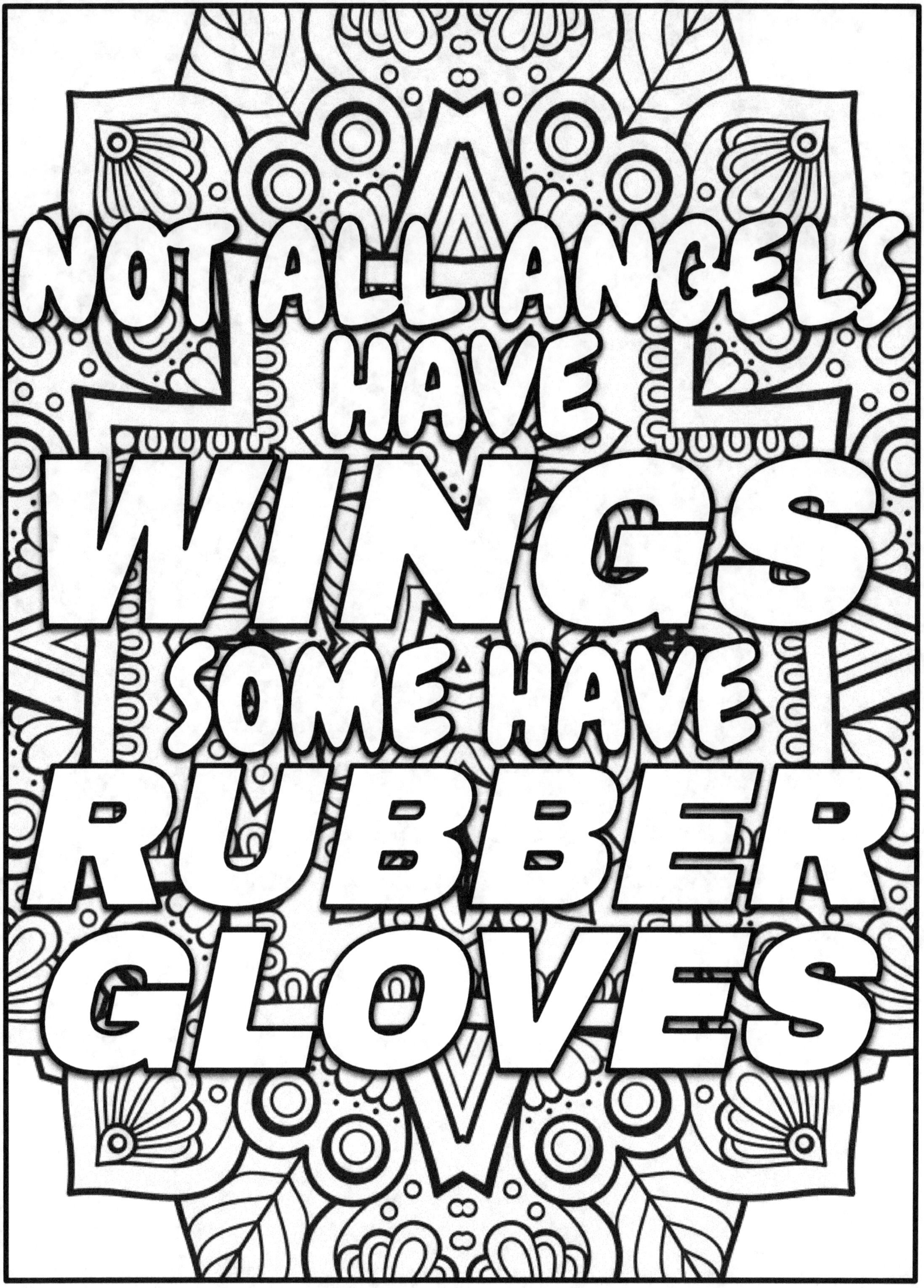
NOT ALL ANGELS
HAVE
WINGS
SOME HAVE
RUBBER
GLOVES

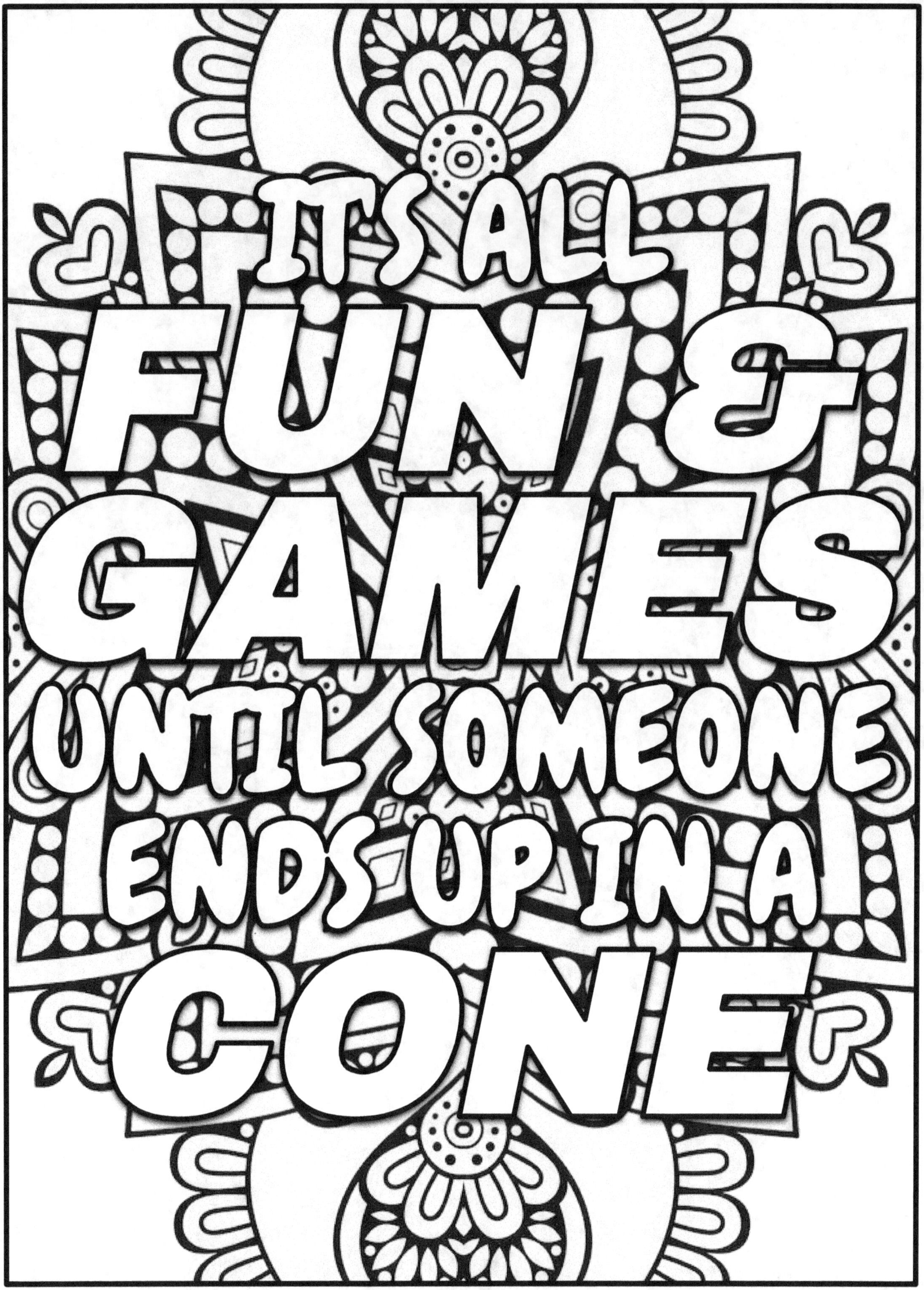
ITS ALL
FUN &
GAMES
UNTIL SOMEONE
ENDS UP IN A
CONE

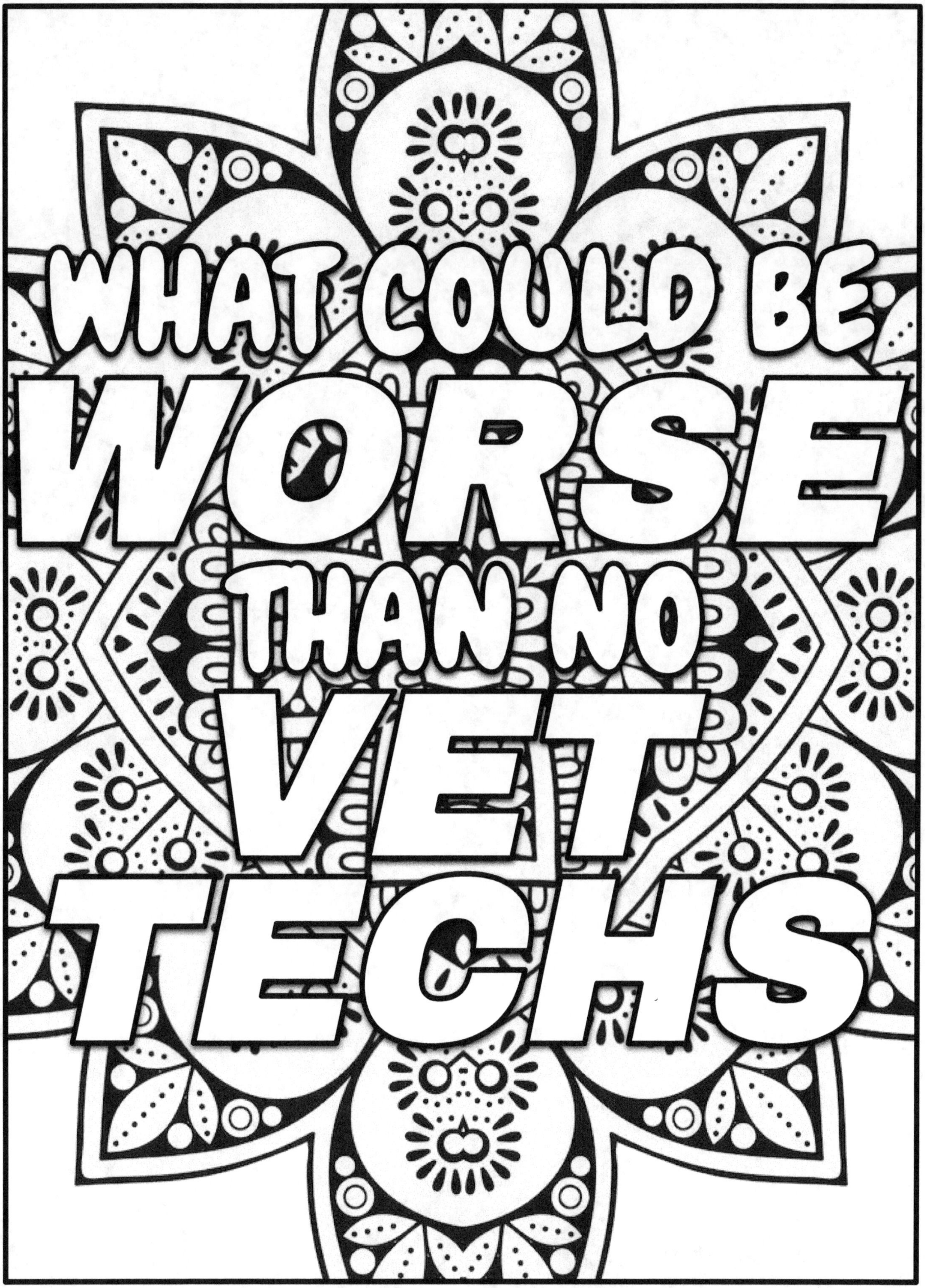
WHAT COULD BE
WORSE
THAN NO
VET
TECHS

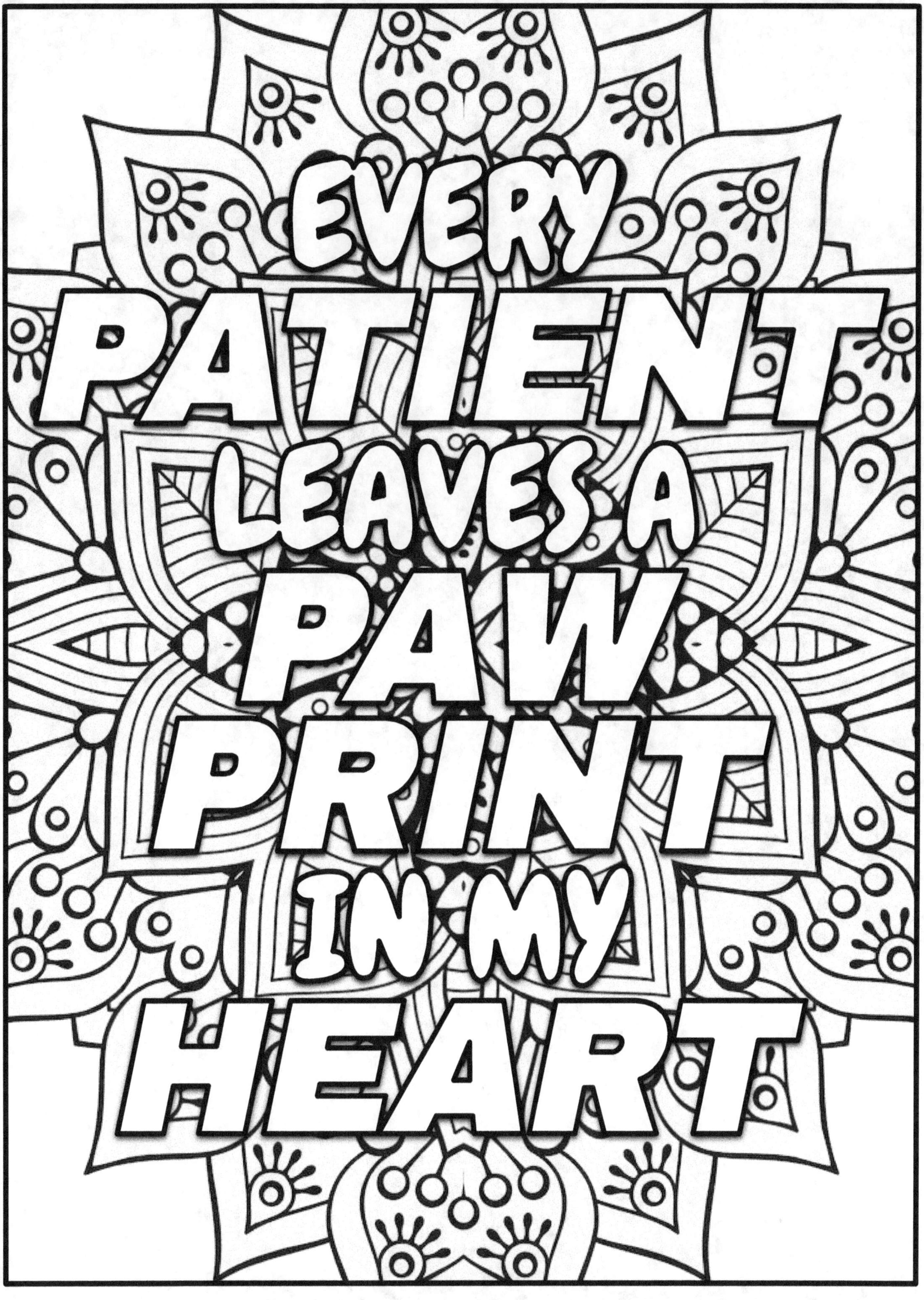
EVERY
PATIENT
LEAVES A
PAW
PRINT
IN MY
HEART

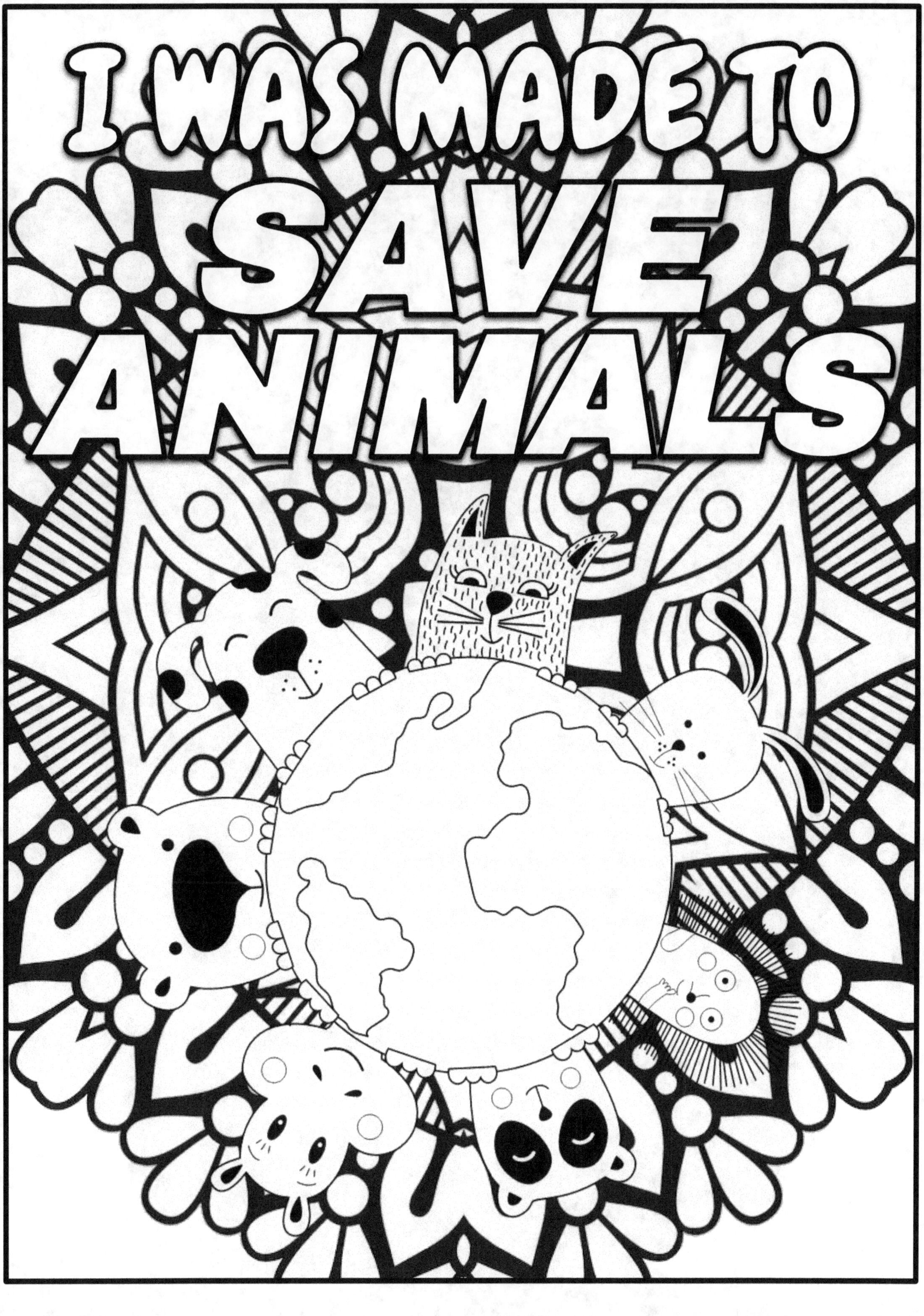
I WAS MADE TO
SAVE
ANIMALS

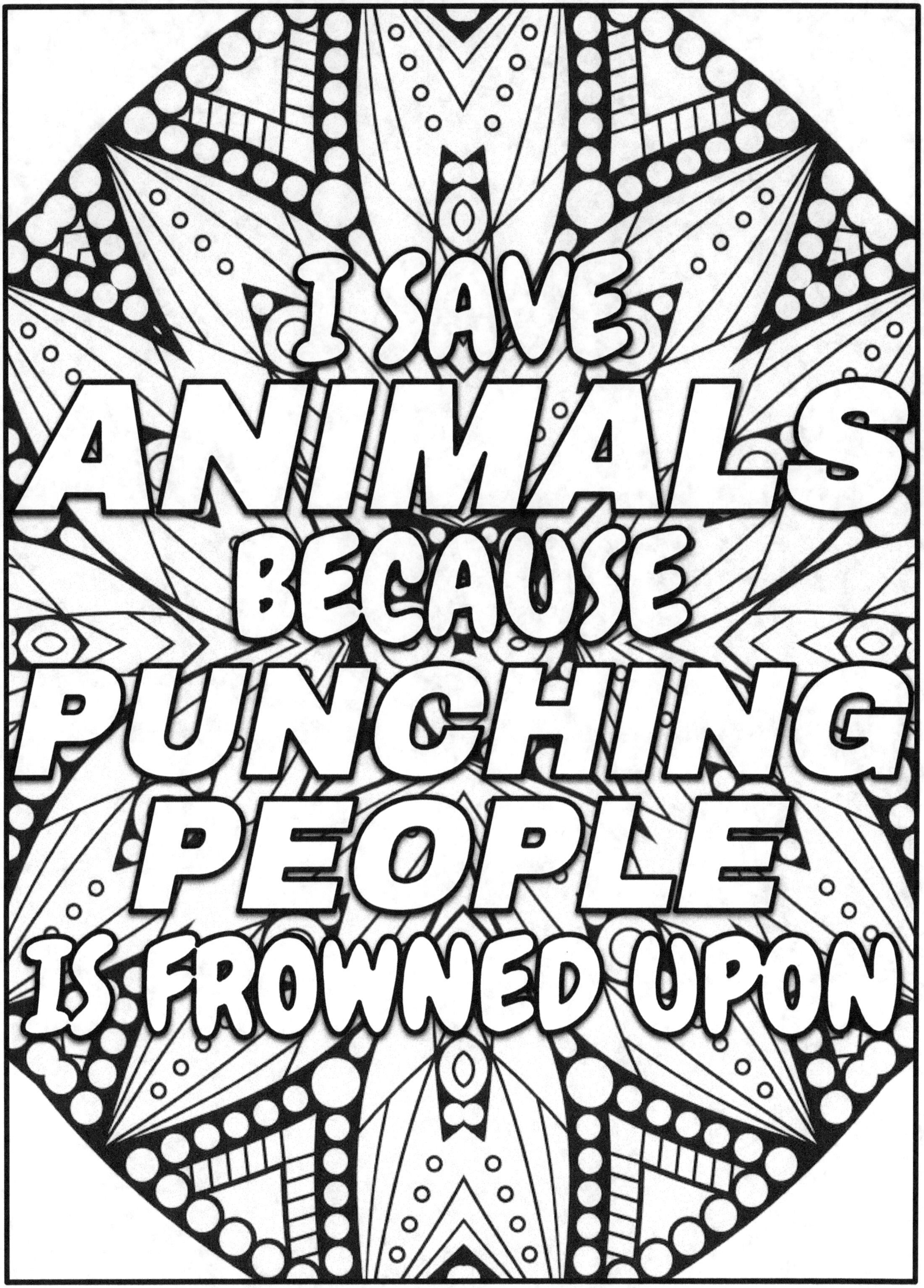
I SAVE
ANIMALS
BECAUSE
PUNCHING
PEOPLE
IS FROWNED UPON

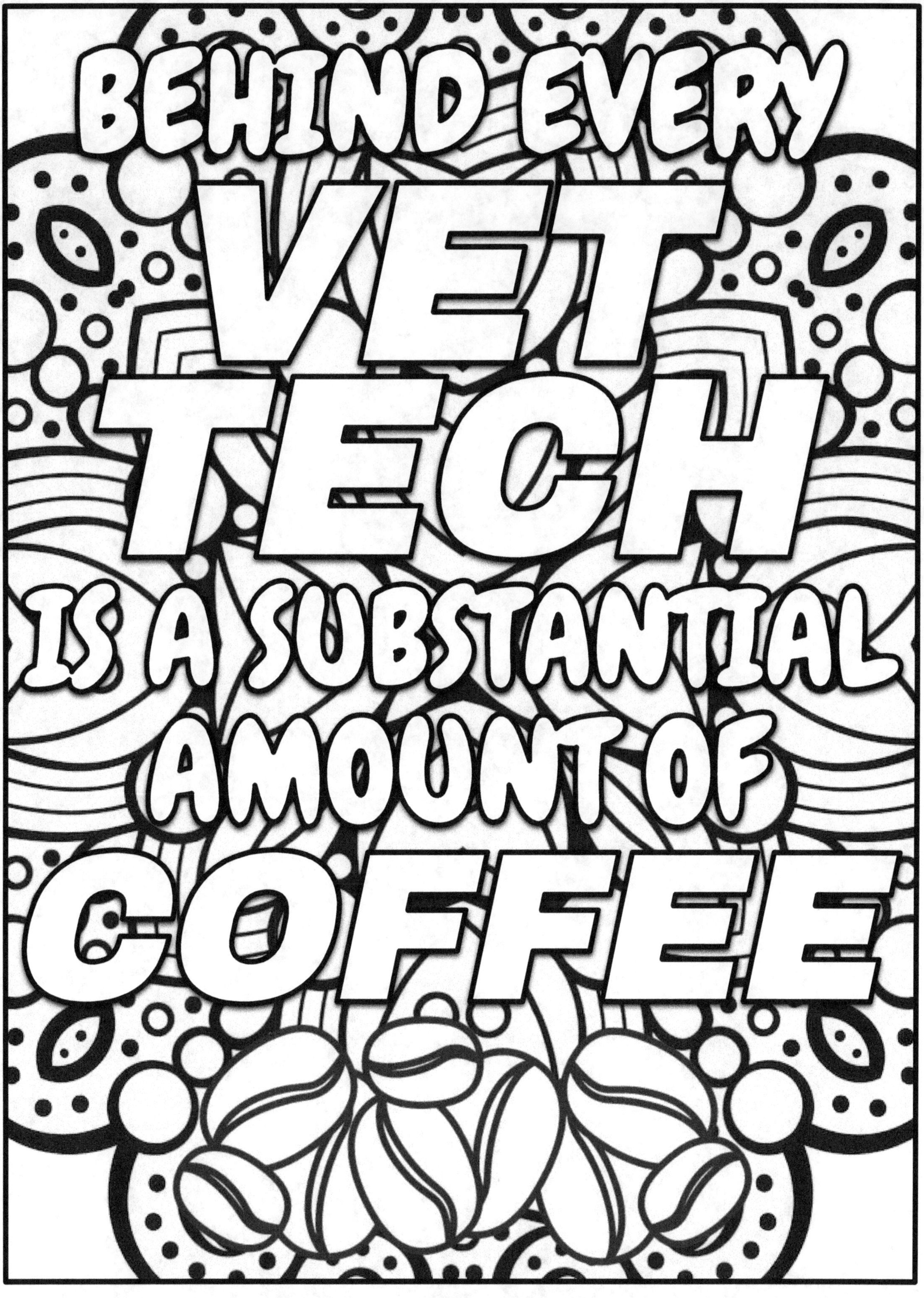
BEHIND EVERY
VET
TECH
IS A SUBSTANTIAL
AMOUNT OF
COFFEE

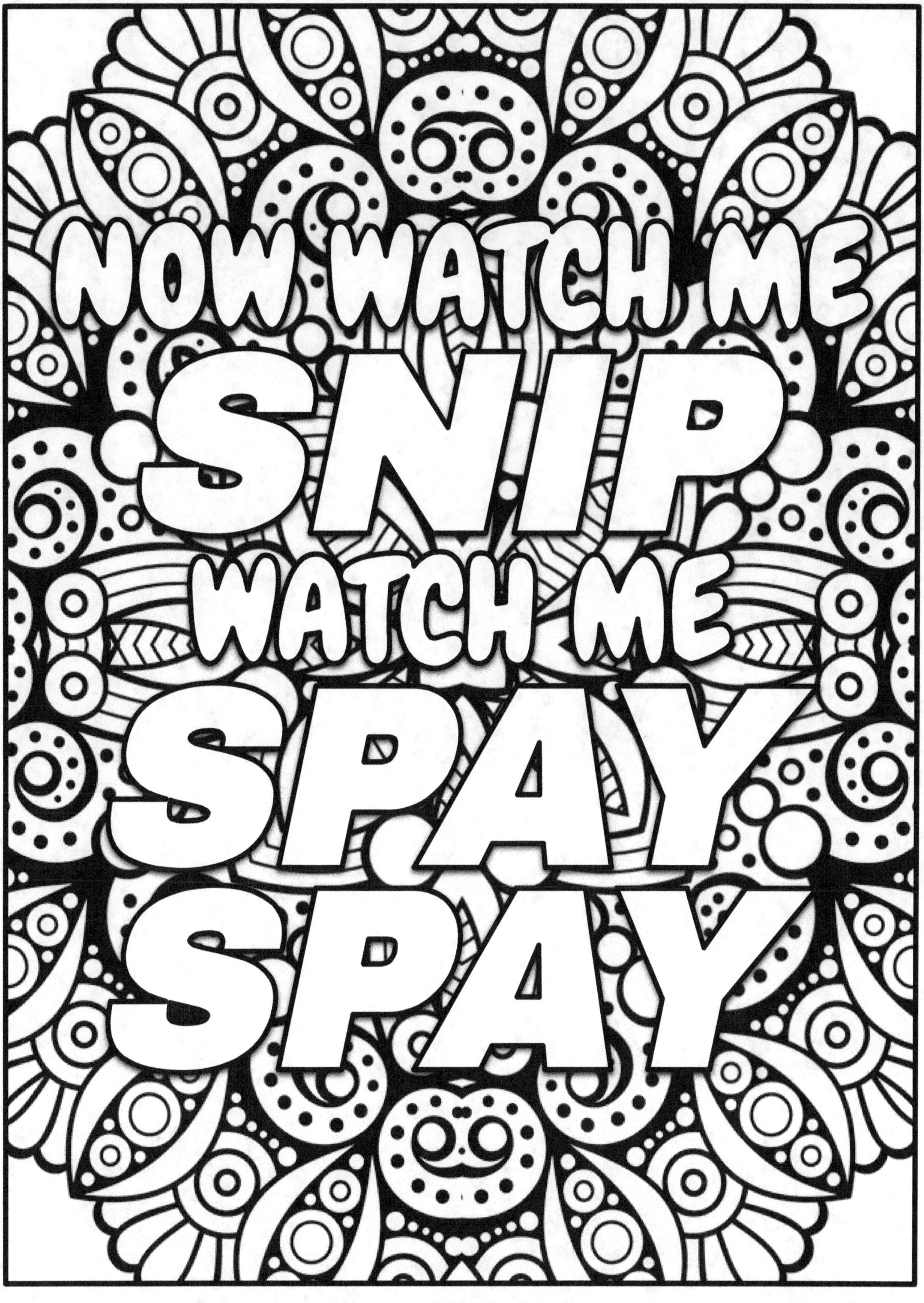
NOW WATCH ME
SNIP
WATCH ME
SPAY
SPAY

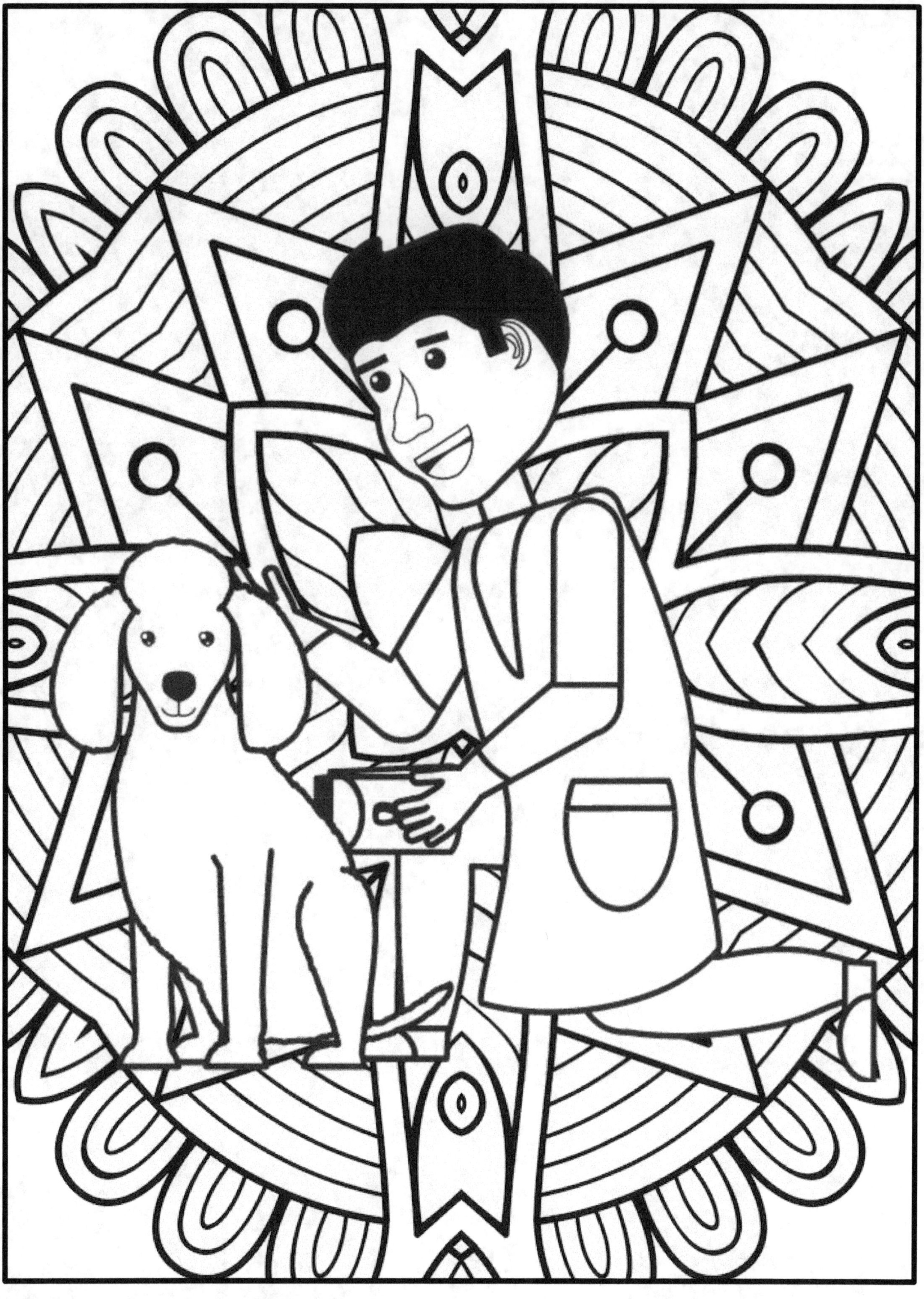

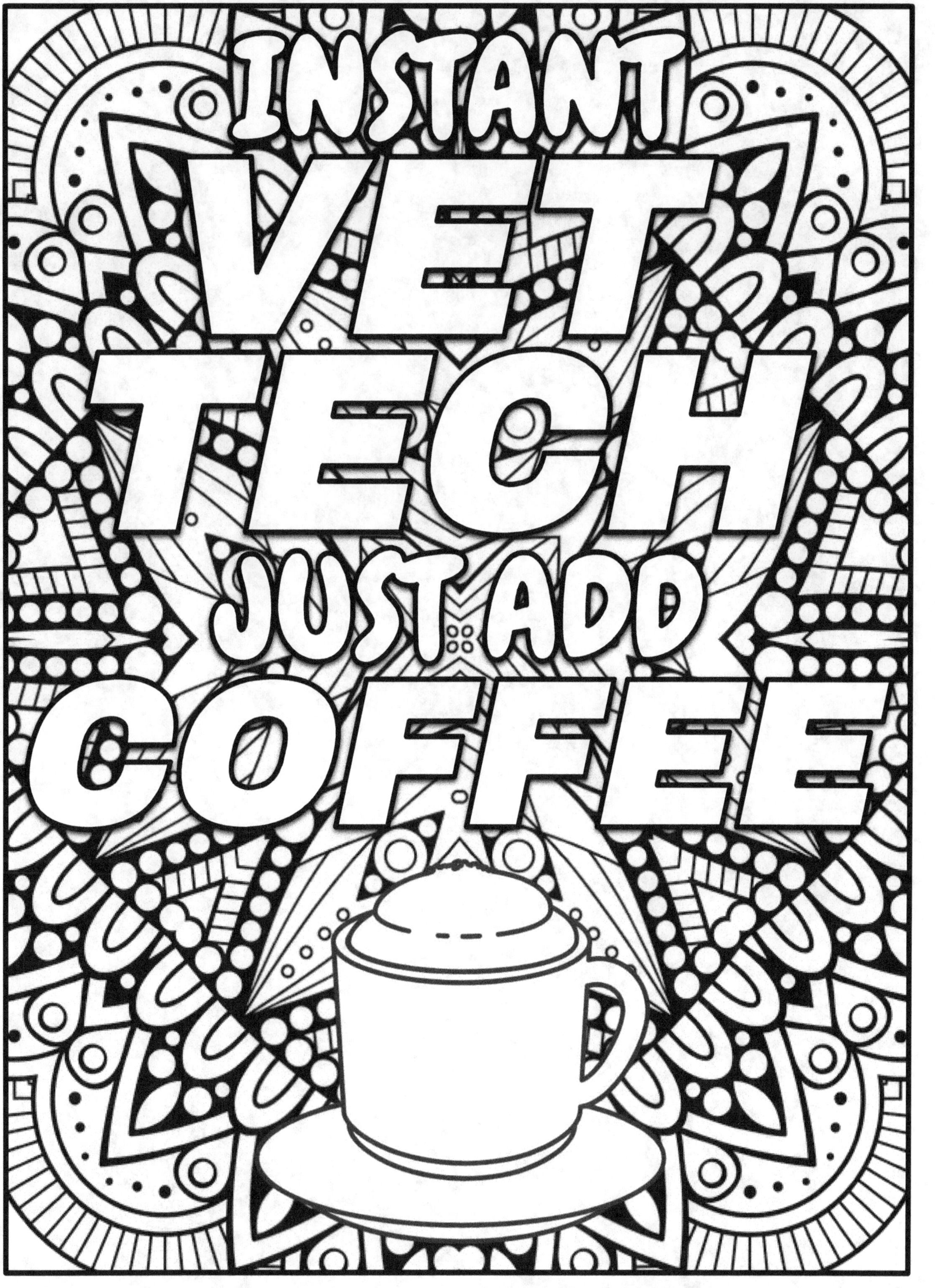
INSTANT
VET
TECH
JUST ADD
COFFEE

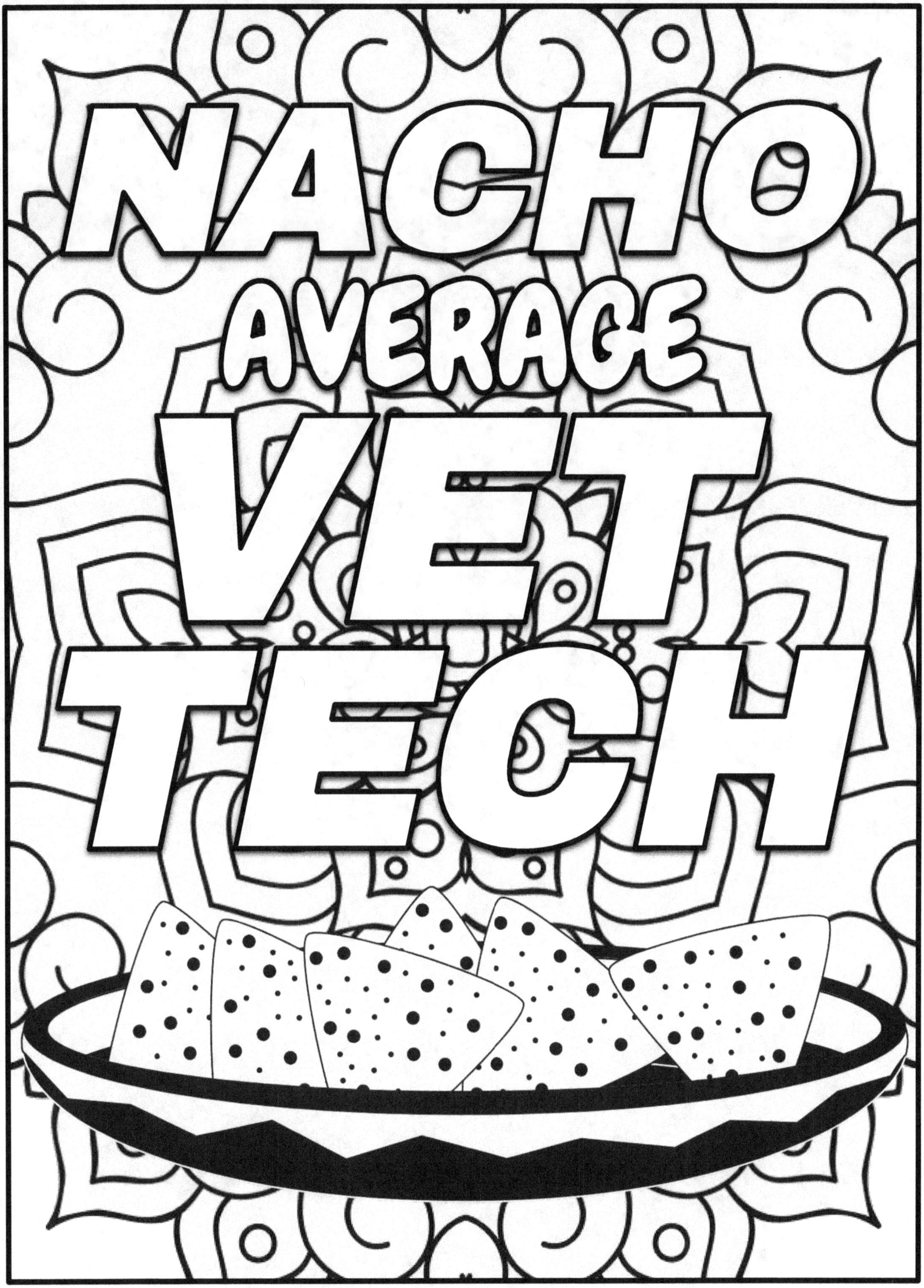
NACHO
AVERAGE
VET
TECH

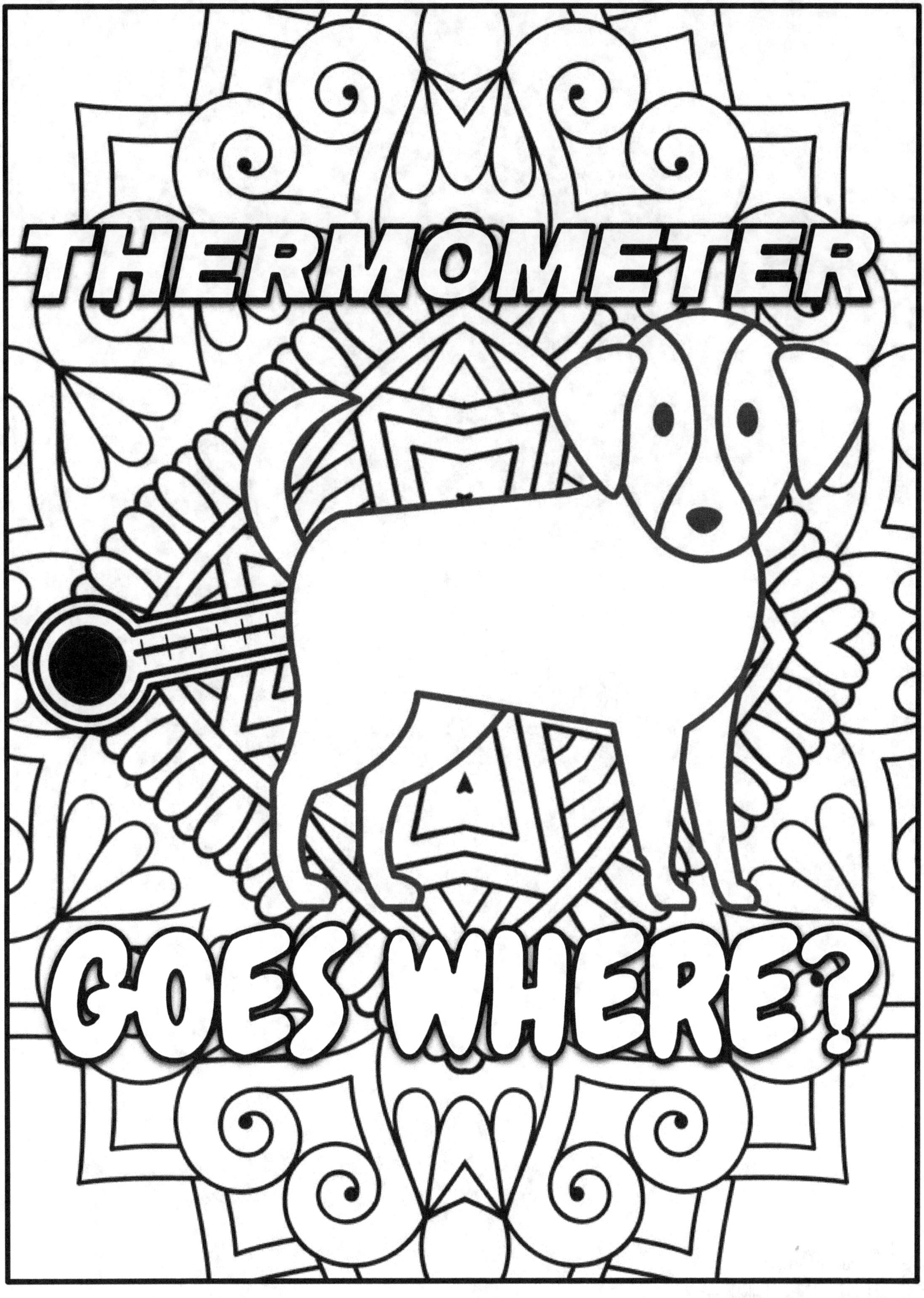
THERMOMETER
GOES WHERE?

www.ingramcontent.com/pod-product-compliance
Lightning Source LLC
Chambersburg PA
CBHW081534220526
45467CB00010B/3182
9798718513783